WeightWatchers®
momentum™

Healthy & Happy Celebrations

135 Recipes, **Entertaining** Ideas & Tips, Easy **Menus**

About Weight Watchers

Weight Watchers International, Inc., is the world's leading provider of weight-management services, operating globally through a network of company-owned and franchise operations. Weight Watchers holds over 50,000 weekly meetings worldwide, at which members receive group support and education about healthful eating patterns, behavior modification, and physical activity. Weight-loss and weight-management results vary by individual. We recommend that you attend Weight Watchers meetings to benefit from the supportive environment you'll find there and follow the comprehensive Weight Watchers program, which includes a food plan, an activity plan, and a behavioral component. In addition, Weight Watchers offers a wide range of products, publications, and programs for people interested in weight loss and weight control. For the Weight Watchers meeting nearest you, call **1-800-651-6000.** For information about bringing Weight Watchers to your workplace, call **1-800-8AT-WORK.** Also visit us at our Web site, **WeightWatchers.com,** and look for ***Weight Watchers Magazine*** at your newsstand or in your meeting room.

FROM TOP LEFT, CLOCKWISE: WATERMELON LEMONADE, PAGE 48; CORN ON THE COB WITH CHILI AND CILANTRO, PAGE 54; AND JAMAICAN JERK PORK TENDERLOIN WITH PINEAPPLE SALSA, PAGE 51.

Weight Watchers Publishing Group

Editorial Director
NANCY GAGLIARDI

Food Editor
EILEEN RUNYAN

Editors
ALICE THOMPSON
CAROL PRAGER

Managing Editor
SARAH WHARTON

Nutrition Consultant
PATTY SANTELLI

Recipe Developers
DAVID BONOM
DEBORAH GOLDSMITH
MAUREEN LUCHEJKO
SARAH REYNOLDS
ALICE THOMPSON

Editorial Assistant
KRISTINA LUCARELLI

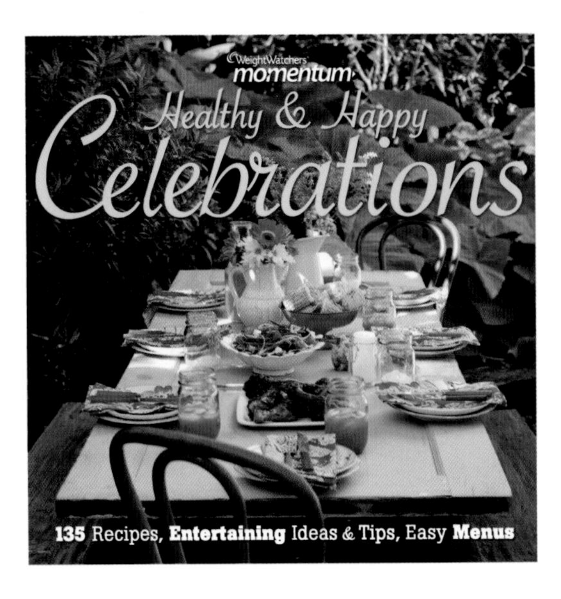

Creative Director
ED MELNITSKY

Photo Editor
DEBORAH HARDT

Production Manager
ALAN BIEDERMAN

Art Director
DANIELA HRITCU

Photographer
KATE SEARS

Food Stylist
LORI POWELL

Prop Stylist
DANI FISHER

Illustrator
DANIELA HRITCU

Consulting Designer
SHELLEY CAMHI

 Editorial and art produced by W/W Twentyfirst Corp., 11 Madison Avenue, New York, NY 10010.

SKU #11182 Printed in the USA

About Our Recipes

We make every effort to ensure that you will have success with our recipes. For best results and for nutritional accuracy, please keep these guidelines in mind:

- Recipes in this book have been developed for members who are following the **Momentum™** plan. We include ***POINTS***® values for every recipe. ***POINTS*** values are assigned based on calories, fat (grams), and fiber (grams) provided for a serving size of a recipe.
- All recipes feature approximate nutritional information; our recipes are analyzed for Calories (Cal), Total Fat (Fat), Saturated Fat (Sat Fat), Trans Fat (Trans Fat), Cholesterol (Chol), Sodium (Sod), Carbohydrates (Carb), Dietary Fiber (Fib), Protein (Prot), and Calcium (Calc).
- Nutritional information for recipes that include meat, poultry, and fish are based on cooked skinless boneless portions (unless otherwise stated), with the fat trimmed.
- We recommend that you buy lean meat and poultry, then trim it of all visible fat before cooking. When poultry is cooked with the skin on, we suggest removing the skin before eating.
- Before serving, divide foods—including any vegetables, accompaniments, or sauce—into portions of equal size according to the designated number of servings per recipe.
- Any substitutions made to the ingredients will alter the "Per serving" nutritional information and may affect the ***POINTS*** value.
- All fresh fruits, vegetables, and greens in recipes should be rinsed before using.
- All ♦™ Filling Extra suggestions have a ***POINTS*** value of ***0*** unless otherwise stated.
- All Filling Foods are indicated with a green icon (♦) in our recipes' ingredient lists.
- Recipes that work with the Simply Filling technique are indicated.

Contents

3 *Fabulous Festivities*

4 *Classic Celebrations*

Introduction

So you're going to give a party? Congratulations! Thanks to ***Healthy & Happy Celebrations,*** you won't have to worry about what to cook: Our collection of delicious menus and recipes is here to help you no matter what the occasion. And because throwing a party—whether it's totally casual or pull-out-all-the-stops fancy—involves some degree of hosting know-how as well, we provide all the information you need. With some easy planning, you can host a party and keep your cool—probably with a lot less work than you think.

The Party Starts Here: Invitations

What does almost every party have in common? Invitations! If you don't extend invitations, you won't have much of a celebration. That said, nowadays a host has a variety of ways in which to do the inviting. Although choice is usually a good thing, it can also provoke some anxiety. Here are the options and the rules you need to know:

Phone, U.S. Mail, or E-Mail? Invitations sent by mail signal a formal event (anything from a sit-down dinner to the celebration of a golden wedding anniversary), whereas a phone call or an e-mail (whether of your own creation or sent via an online invitation Web site, such as evite.com or pingg.com) suggests a more casual affair. Keep in mind that electronic invitations are appropriate only if the people on your guest list check their e-mail regularly (and this may not include your 80-year-old grandmother). If the invitations are going out by mail, be sure to include a response card with a self-addressed, stamped envelope.

The Basics Whichever method you choose, it's a good idea to extend invitations 3 to 4 weeks prior to the party. Be sure to include the date and time of the party, the address, the date by which a response is required (usually a week or so before party day), and a telephone number and/or e-mail address for RSVPs. Also mention suggested attire if the event is formal.

No Reply Yet? The failure of people to respond to an invitation is one of the most frequent complaints that the Emily Post Institute (emilypost.com) receives. According to the Institute, it's perfectly acceptable to call and politely say, "We haven't heard from you, and I'm putting together a final count for the party. We hope you will be joining us."

How Many to Expect For bigger parties, when you've invited acquaintances as well as close friends, a good rule of thumb is to expect 70 to 80 percent of your guests to make it. Most people who are polite enough to RSVP are polite enough to show up (or call if something comes up at the last minute). If someone who hasn't responded arrives, be gracious and make room.

Kids or No Kids? If you prefer not to have children at your party, it's best to deal with this delicate issue in person or by phone, rather than noting it on the invitation. Most guests will realize that a cocktail party or a Saturday-night dinner party isn't a kid-friendly occasion, but if you're concerned that the message isn't clear, you can clarify your position in a phone call. Say something like "It will be so nice for all of us to have some grown-up time for a change" or "I hope you won't have any trouble finding a sitter on a Saturday night."

Party Timing For a weeknight cocktail party, start at 6 or 6:30 p.m. so that guests can come straight from work and go out (or home) for dinner afterward. A Saturday-night cocktail party can start later, say at 7 or 8 p.m. (Cocktail parties at the dinner hour are fine as long as your invitation makes it clear that dinner will not be served.) Weekend dinner parties tend to begin between 7 and 8 p.m. Serving drinks first allows you time to greet your guests as they arrive—and it allows for staggered arrivals; let your invitation convey the details: cocktails at 7 p.m., dinner at 8 p.m.

The All-Purpose Party Checklist

What's the mantra for party success? Plan, plan, plan! That's not a problem with this handy checklist to guide you through the preparation of all your celebrations. Remember: Once you've selected a menu that includes some do-ahead recipes, allow time for making them in your schedule.

☐ 3 TO 4 WEEKS AHEAD

- **Choose a theme—if you want one** Think about a theme in terms of season, guest list, and occasion. Use the theme as inspiration for everything from invitations and decorations to food and drinks. Extend invitations. See The Party Starts Here: Invitations, page 9.
- **Plan the menu** If you aren't going the catering route and you plan to do all (or almost all) of the cooking yourself, we offer one important piece of advice: Keep it simple. Include make-ahead dishes whenever possible (so you don't spend a lot of time running in and out of the kitchen). Another option is to supplement your homemade entrée with takeout or prepared foods (just transfer them to your own serving dishes before placing them on the table).

☐ 2 WEEKS AHEAD

- **Come up with a playlist** The music you select can determine the mood of your gathering. Choose enough to last for the duration of the party, and plan to keep the volume at a level that doesn't hinder conversation.

☐ 1 WEEK AHEAD

- **Clean the house thoroughly** To maintain it for the rest of the week, do a quick cleaning daily.
- **Take stock of tableware, linens, cookware, and serving dishes** Set a mock table to make sure you have everything you need. With a week to spare, you'll have time for a shopping trip if you need to make one. If you're short on an item, consider purchasing an inexpensive version at a discount or thrift store or borrowing what you need—don't be afraid to mix patterns as long as they're compatible. Allocate a serving dish for each item on your menu, and label each dish with a Post-it note.
- **Make a detailed shopping list and cooking schedule** To streamline your shopping route, map out the stores at which you'll buy ingredients and beverages. Place any orders with the butcher, fish market, baker, and liquor store.

☐ 3 DAYS AHEAD

- **Arrange the furniture** Place tables and chairs so traffic can flow freely; remove clutter. Decide on your lighting scheme.
- **Decorate** Lay out all the decorations except the flowers.
- **Designate a place for coats** Make space in a front closet and add a sufficient number of hangers, or designate a bed for coats (and make sure the room is tidy and valuables are out of sight).
- **Shop for food and beverages** Be sure to clean out your fridge before you go shopping, so there is room for all the ingredients.

☐ 1 DAY AHEAD

- **Set the table** See some of our experts' advice, including: Set the Stage: Table Setting and Decorating, page 11; How to Fold a Party Napkin, page 12; and Our No-Fail Dinner Party Seating Plan, page 16. Buy flowers—if you're using them—and arrange them around the house. See also Almost-Instant Centerpieces, page 11.
- **Do as much of the cooking as you can** For foods that require cooking on the day of the party, do as much of the prep (rinsing, chopping, marinating, and so on) as you can.

☐ 1 HOUR AHEAD

- **Be sure the dishwasher is empty** See The Great Cleanup, page 19.
- **Change into your party clothes**

☐ 30 MINUTES AHEAD

- **Take a few minutes for yourself** Get everything ready a little early. Turn on music and light candles or dim lights. Enjoy a glass of wine perhaps, and let yourself be the "guest" for a few minutes.

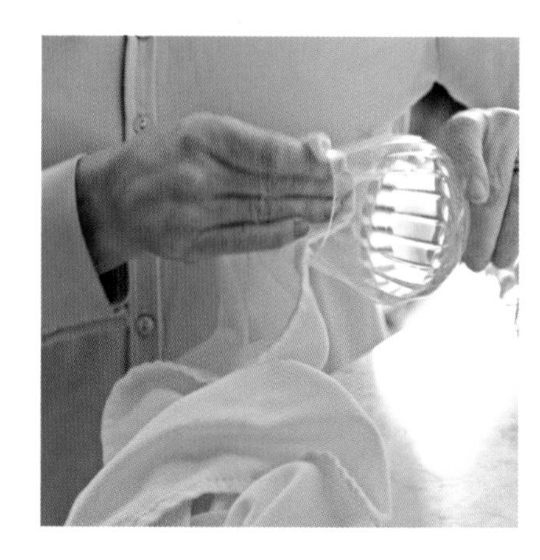

Set the Stage: Table Setting and Decorating

The way you set the table will contribute as much to the ambience of your party as the food or music will. Here are the basic guidelines you'll need for the three most common occasions:

FORMAL SIT-DOWN DINNERS

Even if you're serving a multi-course meal, your table setting need not be complicated (see diagram below). Feel free to express your style by mixing-and-matching sets of china, glassware, and silverware.

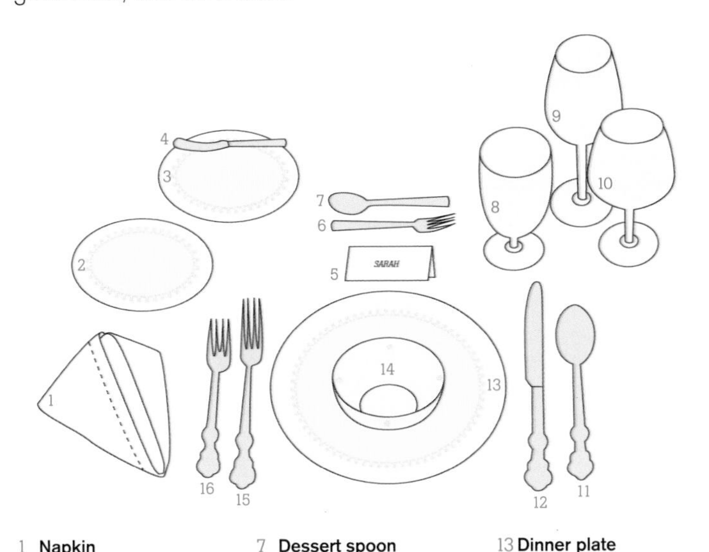

1 **Napkin**
2 **Salad plate**
3 **Bread plate**
4 **Butter knife**
5 **Place card**
6 **Dessert fork**
7 **Dessert spoon**
8 **Water glass**
9 **White wine glass**
10 **Red wine glass**
11 **Soup spoon**
12 **Knife**
13 **Dinner plate**
14 **Soup bowl**
15 **Dinner fork**
16 **Salad fork**

• **China** Formal etiquette dictates that the only china at each place setting at the beginning of the meal is a bread plate and a dinner plate. A first-course soup bowl or salad plate may be set on top of the dinner plate.

• **Silverware** All silverware should be evenly spaced, about a half inch apart, and placed in the order in which it will be used, from the outside in (see diagram above). Dessert utensils are set horizontally above the plate, or they may be brought in later, with the dessert course.

• **Napkins** Make a fancy napkin (see How to Fold a Party Napkin, page 12) and place it on the dinner plate or, if space allows, to the left of the flatware.

• **Glasses** Set each place with all the glasses that will be used during the meal (except those for dessert wine, which may be brought out when dessert is served). People typically reach for water more often than wine, so the water goblet goes above the knife tip, with wineglasses to the right.

ALMOST-INSTANT CENTERPIECES

Looking for some fresh ways to dress up your table?

- **Arrange flowers in small low vases on the table. Avoid flowers with a strong scent, such as lilacs and lilies.**
- **Display big blossoms—like hydrangeas, roses, and peonies—in a soup tureen.**
- **Float apples in water in glass bowls.**
- **Pair smooth objects (such as lemons) with smaller textured ones (such as nuts) in a glass pedestal bowl.**
- **Arrange pinecones in vases of staggered size for winter decor.**

HOW TO FOLD A PARTY NAPKIN

If you think napkin folding is passé, think again. Placing beautifully folded napkins on your table is one of the simplest ways to dress up your decor. To make a classic pyramid napkin, follow these easy instructions—and if you teach the folding part to your kids, they may even become enthusiastic table setters!

1. **Iron napkins with light starch prior to folding.**
2. **Fold the napkin in half diagonally.**
3. **Fold the opposite corners so that they meet at the top point.**
4. **Turn the napkin over.**
5. **Fold the napkin in half to form a triangle.**
6. **Pick up the napkin at the center and stand it upright to create a pyramid.**

INFORMAL LUNCHES OR DINNERS

A casual meal offers a chance to relax and have a little fun, so all you'll need are the basics. Take the opportunity to show a bit of personality by varying textures, patterns, and colors. Here are a few points to keep in mind:

- Flatware aligns more or less with the bottom of the dinner plate.
- Tumblers may be used in place of wineglasses. It's also okay to pair stemmed glasses with stemless.
- Salt and pepper shakers should be placed near the center of the table. If someone asks for the salt, pass the pepper too.

BUFFETS

Although there's no "proper" way to set a buffet table, it's important that the right flow is ensured, from the placement of silverware to the order of the dishes served, so that your guests don't feel as though they're standing on line in a cafeteria.

- Place a stack of plates at one end of the table (or, for large events, at both ends) so that guests pick a plate up first. Choose plates with some heft (avoid flimsy paper plates) and a substantial lip so that food won't slide off easily.
- Arrange serving dishes at different heights, with taller items placed behind shallower ones, so that guests can see and reach everything with ease. Platters and shallow bowls are the most user-friendly choices.
- Roll flatware in napkins to minimize the balancing act. Secure the packets with a bit of twine and pile them toward the end of the buffet. Use sleek flatware; decorative styles are often too bulky to be neatly rolled up.
- Create a beverage bar at a separate station.

Cocktails and Wine Q & A

Q How much alcohol, and what kind, should I have on hand for a cocktail party?

A Rather than stock a full bar, offer a short list of red and white wines, one specialty cocktail (preferably something simple), and one nonalcoholic beverage, such as cranberry juice and sparkling water. Mix up a large batch of the house drink and store it in a big container in the refrigerator, refilling pitchers as needed. Prop up signs to let guests know what they're pouring, and plan on serving 3 to 4 drinks per person for a 2- to 3-hour party. Stock some beer, too, if that's appropriate for your crowd.

Q When should I splurge on a bartender?

A Consider hiring a bartender if you're expecting 25 or more guests. A professional behind the bar will expedite service, eliminate messy amateur drink mixing, and allow you to concentrate on your guests and the food. The price of bartending services varies by region; you can expect to pay between $15 and $25 an hour plus a tip.

Q What's the best way to choose wine for a dinner party?

A Food and wine should work seamlessly together, so choose a wine that mirrors the dish you're making. If you're unsure about wines, ask advice from a wine merchant. If your dish is light and fresh with lots of herbal flavors, for example, ask the merchant for a wine with similar qualities.

Q How much wine will I need for a dinner party?

A Figure 2 to 3 glasses per person. There are at least 4 glasses per bottle, so you'll need 2 to 3 bottles for every 4 guests. Fine-tune this formula based on what you know about your guests' drinking habits.

Q What can I do if I forget to chill the white wine?

A Put the bottle in a bucket half-filled with ice, water, and a large handful of salt. The salt reduces the freezing point of the water and allows it to become super-chilled quickly, so the bottle of wine should chill in about 20 minutes.

Q I made a dish with wine. May I serve the rest of the bottle to my guests?

A Yes—with one proviso. Wine used as an ingredient in a dish should always be high quality, just like any other ingredient in the dish. So when buying wine for a recipe, choose one that you and your guests will enjoy drinking.

Q Is it worthwhile to rent glasses?

A There are several advantages to renting glasses—even for a relatively small party. First, you don't have to worry about having enough glasses. Second, the glasses will be delivered clean and ready to use. Third, you can return the glasses dirty, since the rental company washes them. Most party rental companies rent wineglasses for a low fee (starting at less than $1 per glass).

Q How do I deal with leftover wine?

A Whether the wine is red or white, it's best to recork an opened bottle and refrigerate it to preserve freshness. White wine will be ready to enjoy straight from the fridge. For red wine, you'll want to let it warm to room temperature. As a general rule, opened wines remain in good shape up to 3 days.

Party for Less

Want to feed your friends well without taking too big a bite out of your budget? Party on with these cost-saving tips:

- **Make it a BYOB** There's no need to foot the bill for the wine as well as the food. If guests offer to bring something, ask them to bring wine, beer, or soda. If you're asking for wine or beer, you might even request a particular type or brand to go with the menu. In any case, have a backup stash of your own.
- **Start with bread and cheese** Instead of fancy crackers, dress up a tray with whole-grain baguette slices (fresh or toasted). Stick with affordable domestic cheeses, such as varieties of Parmesan, Gouda, and Cheddar, all of which cost less than $10 a pound. Don't serve boulder-size hunks for appetizers; 3/4 ounce per person is sufficient. Garnish the platter with whatever fresh fruit is in season, such as a few raspberries, grapes, or strawberries in spring; apricot, plum, and nectarine wedges in summer; apple and pear slices in fall and winter; or whatever you can get at a good price.
- **Host a brunch** Eggs and veggies are cheaper than steak any day (see New Year's Day Brunch, page 22, or Mother's Day Brunch, page 92). An egg casserole or vegetarian entrée is a great choice for feeding a crowd.
- **Keep your sweets simple** Scatter orange segments garnished with chopped dark chocolate on a platter and let everyone dig in.
- **Skip costly serving pieces** Serve hors d'oeuvres on a rustic wooden cutting board. Bring braised meat or a hearty pasta dish to the table in a Dutch oven. Serving food family-style creates a bountiful and comforting aura.
- **Do decor on a dime** No need to spend a fortune on flowers. Monochromatic arrangements of inexpensive flowers that are in season—like tulips, daisies, or chrysanthemums—are easy to make and can look elegant. Use lighting to set the mood: Low-watt light bulbs or candlelight will do the trick. Dim the lights and cluster several tea-light candles in votive glasses on a tabletop in your welcome area.
- **Set the table with a personal touch** Be creative: Use seashells from your beach vacation or Grandma's antique holiday ornaments as table decor.

Our No-Fail Dinner-Party Seating Plan

You've received your RSVPs, the table looks fabulous, and a delicious meal awaits. Only one thing remains to ensure a truly smashing evening: the seating plan. Here are three simple rules for placing your guests around the table:

1 Even your dearest family members and friends have their idiosyncrasies. Start by noting each guest's personality traits. Is your cousin shy? Seat her next to a charming, chatty guest who will bring her out of her shell. Does your best friend's husband monopolize a conversation or gossip too much? Place him far from the guest who voices strong opinions freely.

2 Consider yourself the conductor of the evening. Seat yourself close enough to the kitchen that you can clear plates, pass out the next course, and uncork the wine without disturbing your guests. Be sure you are seated in a place where you can easily deal with your guests' needs and manage any problems.

3 Assign your guests to their places. Once you've determined who will click and who will clash, you may want to use place cards to direct your dinner guests to their assigned seats.

PARTY SMARTS: 5 JOBS WORTH DELEGATING

Feeling harried? Next time a guest or family member asks to help, assign him or her one of these easy, fun tasks:

1 Bringing edibles **If a guest offers to bring something from his or her kitchen, take advantage of the offer! Suggest something simple, like a fruit platter, a plate of crudités, or a platter of homemade cookies.**

2 Checking coats **Assign this task to kids or an early arrival so you won't have to run between the front door and the closet or bedroom all evening.**

3 Tending bar **For events with 25 or more guests, appoint someone to serve as the bartender, or set up a self-serve bar and designate someone to do simple bar tasks like clearing away empty wine bottles and replenishing ice cubes and glassware supplies.**

4 Lighting candles and filling water glasses **If you're serving a sit-down dinner, enlist a helper to put the finishing touches on the table just before you're ready to seat everyone.**

5 Making coffee **Prepare the coffee maker ahead of time, and put a guest in charge of starting the machine after dinner and delivering the cups to the table. Have the milk and sugar ready to go, and show your helper where they're stashed.**

Take It Outside

What's better than throwing a pool party or a BBQ in your own backyard on a warm day or balmy evening? But just because the location seems like the same old place to you doesn't mean you have to settle for the same old ambience. Here are 10 suggestions for setting the mood:

1 Create a summer home for dishes. Station an armoire on a covered patio or clear a few shelves in the garage to hold supplies devoted to alfresco dining. Affordable, unbreakable brightly hued enamelware; sturdy flea market finds; or eco-friendly, reusable bamboo plates are good to have on hand.

2 Lay kraft paper across a table for a casually finished look and super-easy cleanup. Keep crayons nearby for creative guests, young and old.

3 Accommodate a large group for an outside sit-down meal by topping two or more folding tables with a rustic flat-paneled door or a single sheet of plywood covered with a cloth.

4 Bring the seashore to your backyard by filling colorful buckets with sand. Fill others with sunflowers.

5 Tackle grill-related tasks ahead of time. Stock up on charcoal or refill the propane tank a week or more before the party. Clean and season the grill rack the morning of your party, and place a sturdy table nearby to hold the grilling tools and serving platters you'll need.

6 Pamper guests at barbecues, clambakes, and other messy, hands-on events by providing dampened paper towels or cloths that have been sprinkled with lemon juice and rolled up, a soothing remedy for sticky fingers.

7 Run a fan near your dining area to keep mosquitoes at bay—and to keep your guests cool. You may also want to stand a container of natural insect repellent in a flowerpot.

8 Set up multiple beverage stations to help your guests stay well hydrated. Galvanized tubs, colorful enamel buckets, and planters work perfectly. Place an assortment of drinks in each bin if they're destined for different locations. If need be, use a ribbon to tether a bottle opener to each bin, and drape a kitchen towel nearby to take care of condensation.

9 Enjoy candlelight on breezy evenings by using hurricane lanterns or jam jars to shield the flames. Or consider battery-operated candles: They provide the same warm light without the worries of wind or dripping wax.

10 Circle your party area with citronella candles or incense sticks to light as night falls and insects arrive.

Eight Rules for Feeding a Crowd

Planning a big bash? You want to avoid cooking for days and days beforehand, and you don't want to run out of food or be left eating leftovers for weeks. Here are hassle-saving hints for pulling off any crowd-pleasing festivity with ease:

1 **Include just one "star" dish** Devote your energy to one spectacular recipe; keep the other dishes on your party's menu simple and straightforward.

2 **Minimize the number of ingredients** Save on shopping and prep time (and free up counter space, which is always at a premium when you're entertaining) by choosing recipes with shorter lists of ingredients.

3 **Keep your cool** Opt for recipes that offer leeway on the serving temperature. Trying to serve 30 guests piping-hot food or worrying about whether your ice-cream dessert will melt is likely to be stressful.

4 **Use this hors d'oeuvres calculator** If you're serving a meal, allow 4 to 6 hors d'oeuvres per guest. If you're serving only hors d'oeuvres and cocktails, count on at least 12 pieces for each guest.

5 **Don't overdo the protein** As a general rule, allow 1/4 to 1/3 pound boneless meat, poultry, or fish per person. If you're serving a whole turkey, however, you'll want to plan on cooking about 1 pound raw bird per person.

6 **Be sides savvy** Estimate about 1/2 cup vegetables, rice, pasta, or stuffing per guest. For salads, estimate 1 to 2 cups per person, and have 2 to 4 tablespoons of condiments like cranberry sauce or haroset on hand for each guest.

7 **Think veggie** Unless you know otherwise, assume you'll have at least one vegetarian guest. Make sure to have one hearty meatless option available. Also consider tweaking recipes for dishes like soups or salads so they contain only meatless stocks and ingredients.

8 **If you're not a baker, consider outsourcing dessert** A cake or pastries from your favorite bakery, along with a fruit salad or platter of fresh fruits, is a perfectly elegant finish to any meal and will free you up to concentrate on the savory courses.

The Great Cleanup

Even the most experienced host dreads the post-party messy house and pile of dishes in the sink. How to tackle the job? Simply break down the tasks and prioritize. Follow this plan and you won't feel overwhelmed:

BEFORE THE PARTY

- Designate an area on your kitchen counter for dirty dishes to be stacked neatly throughout the party. Avoid the pitfall of piling them in the sink while the party is in full swing.
- Place a heavy-duty plastic container next to the dish area for utensils (to minimize the likelihood of their being accidentally dropped into the trash).
- Double- or triple-line the kitchen trash can so that you have a clean bag in place when each full one is removed.
- Have your kids or spouse unload the dishwasher before the guests arrive so the machine will be empty and ready to go.

DURING THE PARTY

Although common sense may say to wash as you go, it's best to spend minimal time cleaning while you're partying. Part of the job of hosting a party is presenting an easy, graceful style that encourages your guests to relax. That means not rushing to the kitchen to clean up before the guests depart (or trailing them with a Dirt Devil). It's fine to spend a few minutes clearing plates or organizing the kitchen as long as you set your guests up in another room and make sure they are chatting happily.

RIGHT AFTER THE PARTY

- Refrigerate perishable leftovers and pack up doggie bags for guests.
- Scrape the stacked plates and empty half-filled glasses and cups into the kitchen sink. Run a load of dishes if you have time.
- Collect bottles, cups, and glasses; look for spills and deal with them right away.
- Separate recyclables.
- Toss out used paper goods and any plasticware you don't plan on reusing.
- Wash and put away sharp knives; leaving them in the sink or on a crowded counter can be dangerous.
- Gather up the trash in plastic bags, starting in the farthest rooms and working your way toward the kitchen so that you centralize the clutter. Take the garbage out as soon as the bags are filled and tied to prevent accidental leaks and minimize unpleasant odors.
- Squirt grimy pots and pans with dishwashing liquid, and fill them with very hot water. Set them on the stovetop overnight: The extended soaking will make them easier to wash later.

THE MORNING AFTER

- After a good night's sleep, do the dusting and vacuuming, again beginning in the farthest rooms and working your way toward the kitchen.
- Complete the kitchen cleanup. 

THE PARTY'S OVER...

However many upsides there are to throwing a party—the rush of self-satisfaction, the thrill of bringing good friends or family members together, the guaranteed invites to your guests' future bashes—you'll probably be exhausted at the end. So how can you shoo out stragglers without hurting their feelings? Check out our top three tricks:

1 Take a cue from the movie theaters **Turning up the lights gets the move-along message across. (Go ahead and turn off the lights in unoccupied rooms too.)**

2 Start packing away the alcohol **Consider making coffee; the smell of brewing beans sends a subtle sensory message. But refrain from starting a full-fledged cleanup.**

3 Turn the music way down **Or turn it off. As an alternative, create a playlist of "closing time" songs. Guests are sure to get the hint.**

Casual Get-Togethers

CHAPTER 1

New Year's Day Brunch

Hoppin' John Salad with Quinoa

prep 15 MIN   cook 10 MIN   serves 6   level BASIC

- ♦ 1 **cup quinoa**
- 2 **cups water**
- 1/4 **cup lime juice**
- 2 **teaspoons honey**
- 2 **teaspoons olive oil**
- 1/2 **teaspoon salt**
- ♦ 1 **(15 1/2-ounce) can black-eyed peas, rinsed and drained**
- ♦ 1/4 **pound lean ham, diced**
- ♦ 1 **red bell pepper, chopped**
- ♦ 1 **yellow bell pepper, chopped**
- ♦ 4 **scallions, chopped**
- 1/4 **cup chopped fresh cilantro leaves**
- ♦ 1 **jalapeño pepper, seeded and minced**

1 Combine quinoa and water in medium saucepan; bring to boil. Reduce heat and simmer, covered, until most of water has been absorbed, about 10 minutes. Drain and transfer quinoa to large bowl to cool slightly.

2 Meanwhile, whisk together lime juice, honey, oil, and salt in small bowl. Pour mixture over quinoa and toss to coat. Add black-eyed peas, ham, bell peppers, scallions, cilantro, and jalapeño; toss to coat.

Per serving (generous 1 cup): 202 Cal, 4 g Fat, 1 g Sat Fat, 0 g Trans Fat, 7 mg Chol, 493 mg Sod, 33 g Carb, 4 g Fib, 10 g Prot, 37 mg Calc. ***POINTS*** value: ***4.***

♦ FILLING EXTRA

If you've got leftovers or you just want to make this salad more substantial, serve it with diced skinless roast turkey breast; a 1/2 cup per serving will increase the *POINTS* value by *2.*

New Year's Day Brunch
MENU FOR SIX

UP TO 1 MONTH AHEAD

- ☐ Make granita for Pink Grapefruit Granita with Campari and Mint.

2 DAYS AHEAD

- ☐ Combine dry ingredients for Orange–Poppy Seed Muffins and store in zip-close plastic bag at room temperature; combine wet ingredients and refrigerate.
- ☐ Make Cheddar and Corn Spoonbread Casserole; let cool and refrigerate.

1 DAY AHEAD

- ☐ Make Hoppin' John Salad with Quinoa; refrigerate.

EARLY IN THE DAY

- ☐ Bake muffins.

1 HOUR AHEAD

- ☐ Bring salad to room temperature.
- ☐ Make Spiced Apple Skillet Pancake.

LAST MINUTE

- ☐ Reheat spoonbread casserole in microwave.
- ☐ Have mint and Campari ready for serving granita.

Cheddar and Corn Spoonbread Casserole

prep 15 MIN cook/bake 40 MIN serves 6 level INTERMEDIATE

- ♦ **2 cups fat-free milk**
- **1 tablespoon olive oil**
- **1/2 teaspoon salt**
- ♦ **1/2 cup cornmeal**
- ♦ **1 (10-ounce) package frozen corn kernels, thawed**
- ♦ **1/2 cup shredded fat-free Cheddar cheese**
- ♦ **1/2 red bell pepper, minced**
- ♦ **1 jalapeño pepper, seeded and minced**
- ♦ **2 large egg yolks**
- ♦ **4 large egg whites**
- **1/4 teaspoon cream of tartar**

1 Bring milk, oil, and salt to boil in large nonstick saucepan over medium-high heat. Very slowly whisk in cornmeal. Reduce heat, switch to wooden spoon, and cook, stirring, until mixture is thickened and smooth, about 5 minutes. Remove pan from heat and stir in corn, cheese, bell pepper, and jalapeño. Stir egg yolks in one at a time, stirring until blended. Transfer mixture to large bowl and let cool slightly.

2 Preheat oven to 375°F. Spray 8-inch-square baking dish with nonstick spray.

3 With electric mixer on high speed, beat egg whites until foamy; add cream of tartar and beat until soft peaks form. Stir one fourth of egg whites into cornmeal mixture. Fold in remaining egg whites with rubber spatula. Scrape mixture into baking dish; level top. Bake until puffed and cooked through, about 30 minutes.

Per serving (generous 3/4 cup): 185 Cal, 5 g Fat, 1 g Sat Fat, 0 g Trans Fat, 74 mg Chol, 368 mg Sod, 26 g Carb, 2 g Fib, 12 g Prot, 196 mg Calc. ***POINTS*** value: ***4.***

This recipe works with the Simply Filling technique.

Orange–Poppy Seed Muffins

prep 15 MIN bake/microwave 10 MIN serves 24 level INTERMEDIATE

- **1½ cups all-purpose flour**
- **¼ cup whole wheat flour**
- **¼ cup ground flaxseeds**
- **1 tablespoon poppy seeds**
- **2 teaspoons baking powder**
- **½ teaspoon salt**
- **1 cup sugar**
- ♦ **¾ cup fat-free milk**
- **¼ cup canola oil**
- ♦ **1 large egg**
- ♦ **1 large egg white**
- **1 tablespoon grated orange zest**
- **¼ cup orange juice**

1 Preheat oven to 400°F. Spray 24-cup mini-muffin tin with nonstick spray.

2 Whisk together all-purpose flour, whole wheat flour, flaxseeds, poppy seeds, baking powder, salt, and ¾ cup sugar in large bowl. Whisk together milk, oil, egg, egg white, and orange zest in small bowl. Add milk mixture to flour mixture, stirring just until blended.

3 Fill muffin cups evenly with batter. Bake until tops spring back when lightly pressed, 10–15 minutes. Cool muffins in pan on rack.

4 Meanwhile, combine remaining ¼ cup sugar and orange juice in small microwavable bowl. Microwave on High until bubbling, about 1 minute; stir until sugar dissolves. With a wooden skewer, poke a few holes in each muffin. Brush orange mixture over muffins, brushing each a few times to allow juice to seep in. Serve muffins warm or at room temperature.

Per serving (1 muffin): 102 Cal, 4 g Fat, 1 g Sat Fat, 0 g Trans Fat, 9 mg Chol, 90 mg Sod, 17 g Carb, 1 g Fib, 2 g Prot, 28 mg Calc. ***POINTS*** value: ***2.***

ORANGE-POPPY SEED MUFFINS, PAGE 25, AND SPICED APPLE SKILLET PANCAKE

Spiced Apple Skillet Pancake

prep 15 MIN   cook/bake 55 MIN   serves 6   level BASIC

- 1 teaspoon canola oil
- ♦ 2 Golden Delicious apples, peeled, cored, and cut into thin wedges
- 3 tablespoons apple juice or cider
- 1/2 teaspoon cinnamon
- Pinch grated nutmeg
- 2 tablespoons granulated sugar
- ♦ 3/4 cup fat-free milk
- ♦ 1 large egg
- ♦ 1 large egg white
- 2 teaspoons melted butter
- 1/4 teaspoon salt
- 1/2 cup all-purpose flour
- 1 tablespoon confectioners' sugar

1 Heat oil in medium ovenproof skillet , such as cast iron, over medium heat. Add apples, apple juice, cinnamon, nutmeg, and 1 tablespoon granulated sugar. Cook, uncovered, stirring occasionally, until apples are tender and most liquid has evaporated, about 10 minutes.

2 Meanwhile, preheat oven to 400°F. Whisk together milk, egg, egg white, melted butter, salt, and remaining 1 tablespoon granulated sugar in medium bowl. Gradually whisk in flour, whisking until smooth. Pour batter over hot apple mixture. Transfer to oven and bake 20 minutes.

3 Reduce oven temperature to 350°F and continue to bake until pancake is puffed and golden, 15–20 minutes longer. Cool pancake in skillet on rack 10 minutes. Sprinkle top lightly with confectioners' sugar and cut into 6 wedges. Serve warm or at room temperature.

Per serving (1 wedge): 135 Cal, 3 g Fat, 1 g Sat Fat, 0 g Trans Fat, 39 mg Chol, 133 mg Sod, 23 g Carb, 1 g Fib, 4 g Prot, 49 mg Calc. ***POINTS*** value: ***3.***

CHANGE IT UP

For a savory rather than sweet pancake, try this Mushroom Dutch Baby: Omit the apples, apple juice, cinnamon, and sugar. Instead, sauté 1/2 chopped onion and 6 ounces trimmed sliced mushrooms in the oil until tender. Make the batter and bake as above, omitting the confectioners' sugar and garnishing the pancake with chopped fresh herbs. The per-serving *POINTS* value for this variation will be 2.

Pink Grapefruit Granita with Campari and Mint

prep 10 MIN cook NONE serves 6 level BASIC

- **3 cups pink or ruby red grapefruit juice**
- **1 cup boiling water**
- **1/2 cup superfine sugar**
- **1 tablespoon grated lime zest**
- **2 tablespoons Campari**
- **6 mint sprigs**

1 Whisk grapefruit juice, water, sugar, and lime zest in large bowl until sugar dissolves. Pour mixture into 9 x 13-inch baking dish. Cover and freeze until partially frozen, about 2 hours. Remove from freezer and stir with fork, breaking up ice crystals. Cover pan again and return to freezer. Continue to freeze, stirring mixture with fork every 30 minutes, until completely icy, about 3 hours longer.

2 Scoop granita loosely into airtight container and store in freezer up to 1 month. To serve, scoop into glasses. Drizzle each serving with 1 teaspoon Campari and garnish with mint sprig.

Per serving (3/4 cup): 127 Cal, 0 g Fat, 0 g Sat Fat, 0 g Trans Fat, 0 mg Chol, 2 mg Sod, 30 g Carb, 0 g Fib, 1 g Prot, 15 mg Calc. ***POINTS*** value: ***3.***

IN THE KITCHEN

If you can, use freshly squeezed grapefruit juice in this recipe—the flavor will be far superior, without the harsh bitterness that store-bought juice sometimes has. One large grapefruit will yield about 1 cup of juice.

PINK GRAPEFRUIT GRANITA WITH CAMPARI AND MINT

Game-Day Favorites

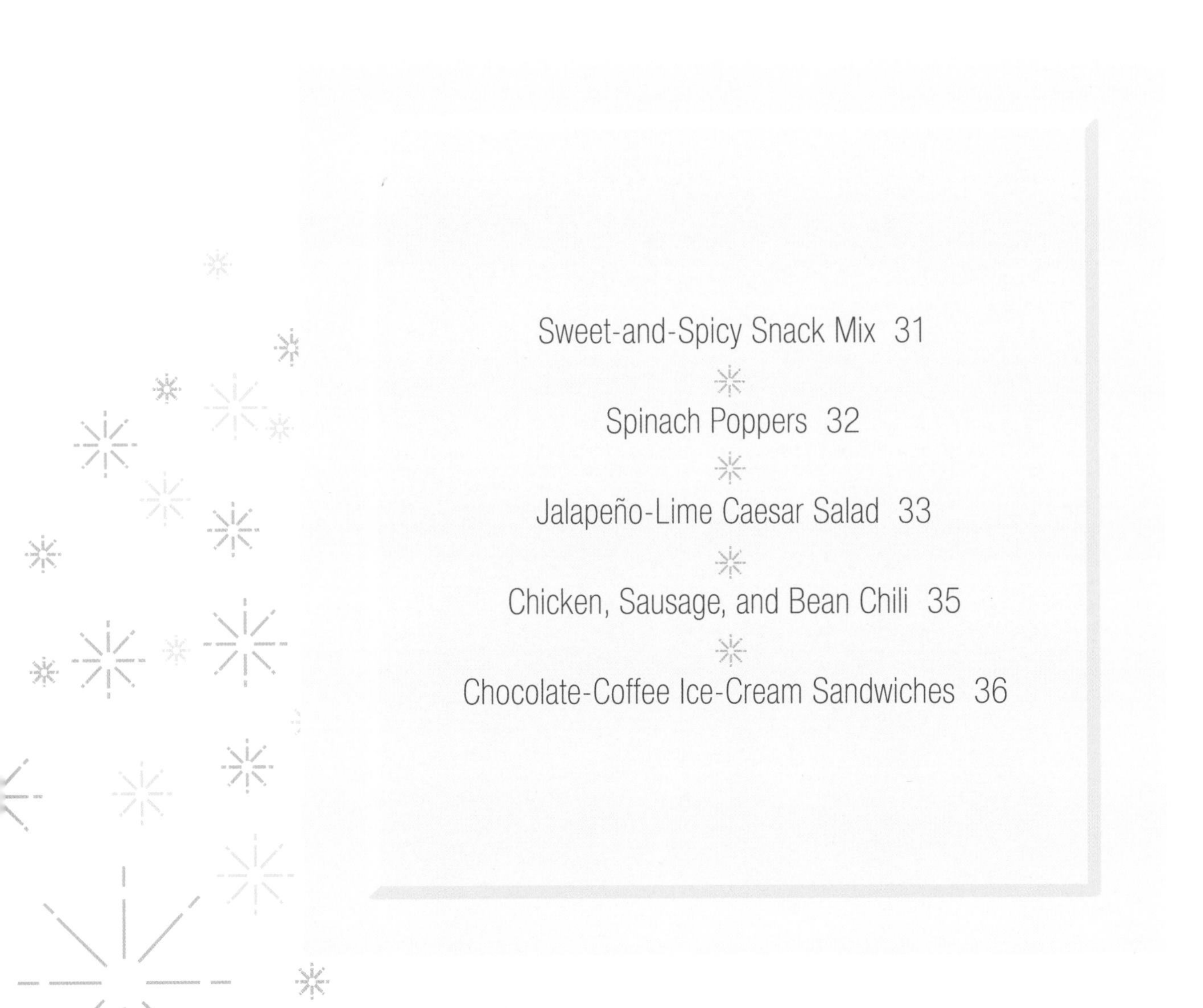

Sweet-and-Spicy Snack Mix

prep 10 MIN cook/bake 45 MIN serves 20 level BASIC

- **3 tablespoons light stick butter**
- **1 tablespoon packed light brown sugar**
- **1 tablespoon Worcestershire sauce**
- **2 teaspoons hot pepper sauce**
- ♦ **6 cups air-popped popcorn (any unpopped kernels discarded)**
- **4 cups corn-cereal squares**
- **3 cups baked tortilla chips, broken into large pieces**
- **2 cups unsalted pretzel twists**
- **1/2 cup lightly salted cocktail peanuts**
- **1 (1 1/4-ounce) package reduced-sodium taco seasoning mix**

1 Preheat oven to 250°F. Spray large shallow roasting pan with nonstick spray.

2 Melt butter in small saucepan over low heat. Stir in brown sugar, Worcestershire sauce, and pepper sauce. Place popcorn, cereal, tortilla chips, pretzels, and peanuts in roasting pan. Drizzle butter mixture over popcorn mixture and sprinkle with taco seasoning. Mix well with wooden spoon. Bake until crisp, stirring occasionally, about 45 minutes.

3 Turn mixture out onto sheet of foil to cool. Store in airtight containers up to 1 week.

Per serving (1/2 cup): 96 Cal, 3 g Fat, 1 g Sat Fat, 0 g Trans Fat, 3 mg Chol, 221 mg Sod, 16 g Carb, 1 g Fib, 2 g Prot, 31 mg Calc. ***POINTS*** value: ***2.***

Game-Day Favorites
MENU FOR SIX

UP TO 1 WEEK AHEAD
- ☐ Prepare Chocolate-Coffee Ice-Cream Sandwiches.
- ☐ Make Sweet-and-Spicy Snack Mix; store in airtight containers.

2 DAYS AHEAD
- ☐ Make Chicken, Sausage, and Bean Chili; refrigerate.
- ☐ Make dressing for Jalapeño-Lime Caesar Salad; refrigerate.

1 DAY AHEAD
- ☐ Make, shape, and coat Spinach Poppers; cover and refrigerate without baking.

1 HOUR AHEAD
- ☐ Finish making salad.
- ☐ Put out bowls of snack mix.

LAST MINUTE
- ☐ Bake poppers.
- ☐ Reheat chili.

Spinach Poppers

prep 30 MIN cook/bake 25 MIN serves 6 level BASIC

- **1 teaspoon olive oil**
- ♦ **1 onion, chopped**
- **1 garlic clove, minced**
- ♦ **1 (10-ounce) package frozen chopped spinach, thawed and squeezed dry**
- **1/2 cup shredded smoked Gouda cheese**
- **1/4 cup finely grated Parmesan cheese**
- ♦ **1 large egg white**
- **1/4 teaspoon salt**
- **2/3 cup plain dried bread crumbs**

1 Preheat oven to 350°F. Spray rimmed baking sheet with nonstick spray.

2 Heat oil in large nonstick skillet over medium heat. Add onion and cook until softened, about 8 minutes. Stir in garlic and cook 1 minute. Let cool 10 minutes.

3 Combine spinach, Gouda, Parmesan, egg white, salt, 1/3 cup bread crumbs, and cooled onion in food processor; pulse until well blended. Shape mixture into about 36 (1-inch) balls. Place remaining 1/3 cup bread crumbs on piece of wax paper and roll balls in crumbs to coat. Place balls 1 inch apart on baking sheet. Bake until firm, about 12 minutes. Serve warm.

Per serving (6 poppers): 128 Cal, 5 g Fat, 3 g Sat Fat, 0 g Trans Fat, 13 mg Chol, 385 mg Sod, 14 g Carb, 2 g Fib, 8 g Prot, 199 mg Calc. ***POINTS*** value: ***3.***

Jalapeño-Lime Caesar Salad

prep 20 MIN cook NONE serves 6 level BASIC

- **1 garlic clove**
- **1/4 cup low-fat mayonnaise**
- **2 tablespoons unseasoned rice vinegar**
- **1 teaspoon grated lime zest**
- **1 tablespoon lime juice**
- **1 teaspoon Dijon mustard**
- ♦ **1 teaspoon minced pickled jalapeño pepper**
- **1/4 teaspoon salt**
- **6 tablespoons finely grated Parmesan cheese**
- ♦ **2 hearts of romaine lettuce, chopped**
- ♦ **1 small carrot, shredded**
- ♦ **1 cup shredded red cabbage**
- **1 cup onion-garlic fat-free croutons**

1 Put garlic in food processor and pulse until minced. Add mayonnaise, vinegar, lime zest and juice, mustard, pickled jalapeño, and salt. Pulse until blended. Add 4 tablespoons Parmesan and pulse to combine.

2 Combine lettuce, carrot, and cabbage in large bowl. Add dressing and toss to coat. Divide salad among 6 plates; sprinkle evenly with croutons and remaining 2 tablespoons Parmesan.

Per serving (2 cups): 81 Cal, 3 g Fat, 1 g Sat Fat, 0 g Trans Fat, 4 mg Chol, 389 mg Sod, 10 g Carb, 2 g Fib, 5 g Prot, 116 mg Calc. ***POINTS*** value: ***1.***

CHANGE IT UP

To make a Mexican-Style Shrimp Caesar Salad, add 3 cups peeled, cooked shrimp to the salad along with the dressing and dust the top of each serving with chili powder. The per-serving *POINTS* value will increase by *1.*

CHICKEN, SAUSAGE, AND BEAN CHILI AND JALAPEÑO-LIME CAESAR SALAD, PAGE 33

Chicken, Sausage, and Bean Chili

prep 25 MIN cook 1 HR 15 MIN serves 6 level BASIC

- 1/2 **pound spicy Italian turkey sausage, casings removed**
- ♦ 1 **pound skinless, boneless chicken thighs, cut into 1-inch pieces**
- ♦ 1 **large onion, chopped**
- ♦ 2 **bell peppers, any color, cut into 1/2-inch dice**
- 3 **large garlic cloves, minced**
- 2 **tablespoons chili powder**
- 1 **tablespoon ground cumin**
- 1/2 **teaspoon salt**
- ♦ 1 **large sweet potato, peeled and cut into 3/4-inch chunks**
- ♦ 1 **(28-ounce) can diced tomatoes**
- ♦ 1 **(15-ounce) can pinto or red kidney beans, rinsed and drained**
- 1 **cup spicy vegetable juice**
- 1 **cup water**

1 Spray 6-quart pot with nonstick spray and set over medium-high heat. Add sausage and cook, breaking up pieces with side of spoon, until browned, about 10 minutes. Transfer to plate.

2 Add chicken to pot and cook, stirring, until browned, about 8 minutes. Stir in onion and cook until softened, about 5 minutes. Stir in bell peppers, garlic, chili powder, cumin, and salt. Cook, stirring, until fragrant, about 1 minute. Add sweet potato, tomatoes, beans, vegetable juice, and water; bring to boil. Reduce heat, cover, and simmer 30 minutes, stirring occasionally. Uncover and simmer until potato is tender and chili thickens slightly, about 15 minutes longer.

Per serving (1 2/3 cups): 298 Cal, 9 g Fat, 3 g Sat Fat, 0 g Trans Fat, 67 mg Chol, 832 mg Sod, 30 g Carb, 8 g Fib, 24 g Prot, 79 mg Calc. ***POINTS*** value: ***6.***

♦ FILLING EXTRA

Add a 15-ounce can of black beans, rinsed and drained, along with the pinto beans and sprinkle each serving of the chili with 2 tablespoons shredded fat-free Cheddar cheese. You'll up the per-serving *POINTS* value by *1.*

Chocolate-Coffee Ice-Cream Sandwiches

prep 30 MIN cook/bake 15 MIN serves 15 level INTERMEDIATE

- **3/4 cup white whole wheat flour**
- **3 tablespoons unsweetened cocoa**
- **1/2 teaspoon baking soda**
- **3/4 cup sugar**
- **5 tablespoons light stick butter**
- **2 tablespoons water**
- **2 ounces unsweetened chocolate, finely chopped**
- ♦ **1 large egg**
- **1 1/2 cups vanilla fat-free ice cream**
- **1 1/2 cups coffee fat-free frozen yogurt**
- **1/4 cup almonds, toasted and chopped**

1 Preheat oven to 350°F. Spray 15 x 10-inch jelly-roll pan with nonstick spray. Line pan with foil, spray again with nonstick spray, and dust lightly with flour.

2 Whisk together flour, cocoa, and baking soda in small bowl. In medium saucepan, combine sugar, butter, and water; bring to boil over medium heat, stirring occasionally. Remove saucepan from heat and stir in chocolate, stirring until chocolate melts; let cool 10 minutes. Whisk in egg; stir in flour mixture. Scrape batter into prepared pan and spread thinly and evenly. Bake until toothpick inserted into center comes out clean, about 12 minutes. Cool in pan on rack, then refrigerate 10 minutes.

3 While brownie layer chills, let ice cream and frozen yogurt sit at room temperature to soften slightly. Turn brownie layer onto cutting board and carefully peel off foil. Cut brownie in half lengthwise, forming 2 rectangles, each 5 x 15 inches. Spread one half with vanilla ice cream and other half with coffee frozen yogurt. Sprinkle ice cream and yogurt evenly with almonds. Sandwich layers together, brownie layers on outside. Cover with plastic wrap and freeze until firm, about 3 hours.

4 Remove plastic wrap and place frozen sandwich on cutting board. With a heavy knife, cut into thirds lengthwise. Slice each third into 5 small rectangular sandwiches. Wrap each sandwich in plastic wrap, place sandwiches in large zip-close plastic freezer bag, and freeze up to 1 week.

Per serving (1 sandwich): 151 Cal, 6 g Fat, 3 g Sat Fat, 0 g Trans Fat, 21 mg Chol, 69 mg Sod, 24 g Carb, 2 g Fib, 4 g Prot, 53 mg Calc. ***POINTS*** value: ***3.***

IN THE KITCHEN

Wondering what white whole wheat flour is? Regular whole wheat flour is typically milled from red wheat, whereas white whole wheat flour is milled from white wheat, resulting in a lighter, less strongly flavored flour. Use it to work more whole grains into your baking.

CHOCOLATE-COFFEE ICE-CREAM SANDWICHES

Memorial Day Cookout

Arugula Salad with Toasted Walnuts and Crisp Bacon

prep 10 MIN cook 10 MIN serves 6 level BASIC

- **4 slices turkey bacon**
- **1 tablespoon olive oil**
- **1 tablespoon balsamic vinegar**
- **1 tablespoon water**
- **1 teaspoon Dijon mustard**
- **1/4 teaspoon salt**
- **1/4 teaspoon black pepper**
- **1 garlic clove, minced**
- ♦ **1 (5-ounce) package baby arugula**
- ♦ **1 head Belgian endive**
- **1/3 cup walnut halves, toasted and coarsely chopped**

1 Cook bacon in medium nonstick skillet over medium heat until browned, about 4 minutes per side. Transfer to paper towels to drain. Crumble when cool.

2 Meanwhile, whisk together oil, vinegar, water, mustard, salt, pepper, and garlic in large salad bowl; add arugula, endive, walnuts, and bacon. Toss to coat.

Per serving (1 cup): 97 Cal, 9 g Fat, 1 g Sat Fat, 0 g Trans Fat, 8 mg Chol, 239 mg Sod, 3 g Carb, 1 g Fib, 3 g Prot, 53 mg Calc. ***POINTS*** value: ***2.***

CHANGE IT UP

Arugula is a classic green for early-summer salads, and it stands up well when dressed ahead of time. If you prefer, you could substitute baby spinach leaves, mixed salad greens, or leaf lettuce for the arugula; the *POINTS* value will remain the same.

Memorial Day Cookout

MENU FOR SIX

3 DAYS AHEAD

- ☐ Make sauce for Grilled Sirloin with Sweet-and-Spicy Coffee; refrigerate.

1 TO 2 DAYS AHEAD

- ☐ Bake your choice of dessert, either Cool Lemon Tart or Cranberry–Chocolate Chunk Cookies (or both!).

EARLY IN THE DAY

- ☐ Give your grill the once-over to make sure it's clean and all supplies and utensils are handy.
- ☐ Cook bacon, toast walnuts, and make dressing for Arugula Salad with Toasted Walnuts and Crisp Bacon; store walnuts at room temperature and refrigerate bacon and dressing separately.
- ☐ Prepare but do not cook packet of Grill-Roasted Fingerling Potatoes; store at room temperature.

1 HOUR AHEAD

- ☐ Preheat grill and start to cook sirloin.

30 MINUTES AHEAD

- ☐ Grill potato packet.
- ☐ Make Sweet Bell Peppers with Olive Vinaigrette.

LAST MINUTE

- ☐ Finish making salad.
- ☐ Toss potatoes with herbs.
- ☐ Carve sirloin.

FROM TOP LEFT, CLOCKWISE: GRILL-ROASTED FINGERLING POTATOES, PAGE 42; ARUGULA SALAD WITH TOASTED WALNUTS AND CRISP BACON, PAGE 39; AND GRILLED SIRLOIN WITH SWEET-AND-SPICY COFFEE SAUCE

Grilled Sirloin with Sweet-and-Spicy Coffee Sauce

prep 10 MIN cook/grill 50 MIN serves 6 level INTERMEDIATE

- **1/2 cup espresso or strong brewed coffee**
- **1/4 cup ketchup**
- **1/4 cup bottled steak sauce**
- **1/4 cup packed light brown sugar**
- **1/4 cup apple cider vinegar**
- **1 tablespoon chili powder**
- **1 tablespoon Dijon mustard**
- **1 tablespoon hot pepper sauce**
- **1 teaspoon ground cumin**
- **1 large garlic clove, minced**
- ♦ **1 (1 1/4-pound) top sirloin steak, 1 1/4 inches thick, trimmed**
- **1/4 teaspoon salt**

1 To prepare sauce, stir espresso, ketchup, steak sauce, brown sugar, vinegar, chili powder, mustard, pepper sauce, cumin, and garlic together in medium saucepan. Bring to boil over medium-high heat, stirring occasionally. Reduce heat to low and simmer, stirring frequently, until sauce thickens, about 20 minutes.

2 Spray grill rack with nonstick spray; preheat grill to medium or prepare medium fire.

3 Sprinkle steak with salt and place on grill rack. Cover grill and cook steak 8 minutes per side. Uncover grill; continue to cook steak, turning and brushing it frequently with half of sauce, until instant-read thermometer inserted into center of steak registers 145°F for medium rare, about 10 minutes longer. Transfer to cutting board and let stand 5 minutes; cut on diagonal into 24 very thin slices. Serve with remaining sauce.

Per serving (4 slices steak and 2 tablespoons sauce): 180 Cal, 5 g Fat, 2 g Sat Fat, 1 g Trans Fat, 53 mg Chol, 552 mg Sod, 16 g Carb, 1 g Fib, 19 g Prot, 40 mg Calc. ***POINTS*** value: ***4.***

CHANGE IT UP

Want a speedier main course? Flank steak makes a good substitute for the sirloin, and since it's a fairly thin cut, you'll need only about 15 minutes total grilling time to produce a medium-rare 1 1/4-pound flank steak. To save even more time, substitute 1 1/2 cups of your favorite store-bought barbecue sauce for the coffee sauce. The per-serving *POINTS* value for these variations will be *3.*

Grill-Roasted Fingerling Potatoes

prep 15 MIN grill 25 MIN serves 6 level BASIC

- ♦ **1 1/2 pounds fingerling potatoes, each halved lengthwise**
- **3 small shallots, thinly sliced**
- **2 teaspoons olive oil**
- **1/2 teaspoon salt**
- **1/4 teaspoon cracked black pepper**
- **1/4 cup chopped fresh dill or 2 teaspoon-chopped fresh rosemary**

1 Spray grill rack with nonstick spray; preheat grill to medium or prepare medium fire.

2 Combine potatoes, shallots, oil, salt, and pepper in medium bowl and toss until evenly coated. Using 18-inch-wide heavy-duty foil, layer two 20 x 18-inch sheets on top of each other to make double thickness. Spray top layer with nonstick spray. Place potato mixture in center of foil. Fold foil into packet, making tight seal.

3 Place packet on grill rack and cook, turning occasionally, until potatoes are fork-tender, about 25 minutes. Open packet carefully (steam will escape), transfer potato mixture to bowl, and toss with dill.

Per serving (2/3 cup): 106 Cal, 2 g Fat, 0 g Sat Fat, 0 g Trans Fat, 0 mg Chol, 204 mg Sod, 21 g Carb, 2 g Fib, 3 g Prot, 19 mg Calc. ***POINTS*** value: ***2.***

IN THE KITCHEN

We call for fingerling potatoes in this recipe because we love their long, thin shapes and diverse flavors and colors. Look for fingerlings at your supermarket or local farmers' market, or substitute any small potato (or a mixture of small potatoes); you can even use medium-size red or gold potatoes if you quarter rather than halve them. This recipe works with the Simply Filling technique.

Sweet Bell Peppers with Olive Vinaigrette

prep 10 MIN grill 10 MIN serves 6 level BASIC

- ♦ **4 bell peppers, any color**
- **4 teaspoons red wine vinegar**
- **2 1/2 teaspoons olive oil**
- **1/4 teaspoon salt**
- **1/4 teaspoon red pepper flakes**
- ♦ **1/3 cup brine-cured pitted Kalamata olives, finely chopped**
- **1 tablespoon water**

1 Spray grill rack with nonstick spray; preheat grill to medium or prepare medium fire.

2 Cut each pepper lengthwise into 6 strips; discard stems and seeds. Stir 2 teaspoons vinegar, 1 1/2 teaspoons oil, salt, and pepper flakes together in medium bowl; add bell peppers and toss to coat. Place peppers on grill rack; cook, turning once, until tender and slightly charred, 10–12 minutes.

3 Meanwhile, stir olives, water, and remaining 2 teaspoons vinegar and 1 teaspoon oil together in small bowl. Place peppers on platter and spoon olive mixture evenly over them.

Per serving (1/2 cup): 46 Cal, 2 g Fat, 0 g Sat Fat, 0 g Trans Fat, 0 mg Chol, 147 mg Sod, 6 g Carb, 2 g Fib, 1 g Prot, 12 mg Calc. ***POINTS*** value: ***1.***

♦ FILLING EXTRA

Top the peppers with chopped cherry tomatoes and sliced basil or oregano leaves for a summery addition. This recipe works with the Simply Filling technique.

Cool Lemon Tart

prep 20 MIN bake/cook 15 MIN serves 10 level INTERMEDIATE

- **7 low-fat honey graham crackers**
- **3 tablespoons melted unsalted butter**
- **1 tablespoon brown sugar**
- **1/3 cup water**
- **1 envelope unflavored gelatin**
- **1 (14-ounce) can fat-free sweetened condensed milk**
- ♦ **1 1/4 cups plain fat-free yogurt**
- **2 teaspoons finely grated lemon zest**
- **1/2 cup lemon juice**
- **Lemon slices and mint leaves (optional)**

1 Preheat oven to 375°F. Put crackers in food processor and pulse to make fine crumbs. Transfer to small bowl and stir in melted butter and brown sugar. Press crumb mixture evenly onto bottom and up sides of 9-inch tart pan with removable bottom, making sure to push mixture all the way to rim. Bake crust until golden, 10–12 minutes. Cool on rack until ready to fill.

2 Meanwhile, pour water into small saucepan; sprinkle gelatin over water and let stand 2 minutes to soften. Set over low heat and cook, stirring frequently, until gelatin dissolves. Remove from heat.

3 Whisk together condensed milk, yogurt, and lemon zest and juice in medium bowl. Gradually whisk in gelatin mixture. Pour mixture into crust. Refrigerate until set, at least 3 hours or up to 1 day. Decorate tart with lemon slices and mint (if using) and cut into 10 wedges.

Per serving (1 wedge): 184 Cal, 4 g Fat, 2 g Sat Fat, 0 g Trans Fat, 12 mg Chol, 81 mg Sod, 33 g Carb, 0 g Fib, 6 g Prot, 155 mg Calc. ***POINTS*** value: ***4***.

CHANGE IT UP

If you're lucky enough to have access to Key limes, substitute 1/2 cup Key lime juice for the lemon juice in this recipe and you'll have a delicious version of that Florida favorite Key lime pie. You'll need up to 20 Key limes to get 1/2 cup of juice (they're tiny!); omit the zest, as the peel of Key limes tends to be bitter. The *POINTS* value will remain the same.

COOL LEMON TART AND CRANBERRY–CHOCOLATE CHUNK COOKIES, PAGE 46

Cranberry–Chocolate Chunk Cookies

prep 15 MIN bake 10 MIN serves 12 level BASIC

- **1/2 cup all-purpose flour**
- ♦ **1/4 cup quick-cooking oats**
- **1/2 teaspoon baking soda**
- **1/8 teaspoon salt**
- **2 tablespoons unsalted butter, melted and cooled**
- **1/3 cup packed light brown sugar**
- ♦ **1 large egg**
- **1 teaspoon vanilla extract**
- **2 ounces semisweet chocolate, cut into 1/4-inch pieces**
- **1/3 cup dried cranberries**

1 Preheat oven to 350°F. Spray large baking sheet with nonstick spray.

2 Combine flour, oats, baking soda, and salt in small bowl; set aside. With electric mixer on low speed, beat melted butter, brown sugar, egg, and vanilla in medium bowl until well blended. Add flour mixture and stir just until combined. Fold in chocolate and cranberries.

3 Drop dough by level tablespoonfuls onto baking sheet, making 12 mounds and leaving 2 inches between them. With bottom of glass dipped in flour or with your fingers, press each mound to make 2-inch rounds. Bake until lightly browned along edges, 9–11 minutes. Cool cookies on baking sheet for 1 minute, then transfer with spatula to rack to cool completely. Store in airtight container up to 2 days.

Per serving (1 cookie): 104 Cal, 4 g Fat, 2 g Sat Fat, 0 g Trans Fat, 23 mg Chol, 85 mg Sod, 16 g Carb, 1 g Fib, 2 g Prot, 12 mg Calc. ***POINTS*** value: **2.**

July 4th Grilling Celebration

July 4th Grilling Celebration
MENU FOR TWELVE

2 DAYS AHEAD
- ☐ Make Watermelon Lemonade; chill.

1 DAY AHEAD
- ☐ Marinate pork for Jamaican Jerk Pork Tenderloin with Pineapple Salsa; prepare salsa without adding basil.
- ☐ Make Wheat Berry Salad with Peas, Bacon, and Tomatoes; refrigerate.
- ☐ Cook and cool beans for Minted Green Bean Salad; wrap in paper towels and then in plastic wrap and refrigerate.
- ☐ Bake Peach Crisp with Spiced Oat Topping; store at room temperature.

EARLY IN THE DAY
- ☐ Give your grill the once-over to make sure it's clean and all supplies and utensils are handy.
- ☐ Make glaze for Grilled Chicken with Balsamic Glaze and refrigerate; coat chicken with spice rub and refrigerate.
- ☐ Shuck corn for Corn on the Cob with Chili and Cilantro, break ears into pieces, and make spice mixture.
- ☐ Finish making green bean salad.

1 HOUR AHEAD
- ☐ Prepare grill; cook pork tenderloins and chicken.

LAST MINUTE
- ☐ Cook corn. Coat in lemon juice, oil, and cilantro; sprinkle with spice mixture.
- ☐ Cut watermelon wedges for lemonade; pour lemonade into glasses, add ice (if using), and garnish.

Watermelon Lemonade

prep 20 MIN cook NONE serves 12 level BASIC

- ♦ **1/2 large seedless watermelon, flesh cut into chunks**
- **3/4 cup lemon juice**
- **1/2 cup sugar**
- **Ice cubes (optional)**
- ♦ **12 small watermelon wedges**

1 Working in batches, puree watermelon chunks in blender or food processor. Strain through mesh sieve into large bowl. Add lemon juice and sugar, stirring until sugar dissolves. Transfer to large pitcher and chill at least 2 hours or up to 2 days.

2 Stir lemonade; pour evenly into 12 glasses. Add ice (if using) and garnish each glass with 1 watermelon wedge.

Per serving (1 cup lemonade and 1 watermelon wedge): 92 Cal, 0 g Fat, 0 g Sat Fat, 0 g Trans Fat, 0 mg Chol, 7 mg Sod, 28 g Carb, 1 g Fib, 1 g Prot, 15 mg Calc. ***POINTS*** value: ***2.***

IN THE KITCHEN
If you'd rather serve this lemonade in a punch bowl, consider filling a medium metal bowl with water and freezing it the day before your party. Just before serving your lemonade, dip the bottom of the metal bowl in hot water to release your giant ice cube, and place it in the bottom of the punch bowl; it will melt slowly, chilling the lemonade but not adding as much water as individual ice cubes would.

Wheat Berry Salad with Peas, Bacon, and Tomatoes

prep 15 MIN cook 1 HR 5 MIN serves 12 level BASIC

- ♦ 1 1/2 cups wheat berries, rinsed
- 4 cups water
- ♦ 6 slices Canadian bacon
- ♦ 2 onions, chopped
- 5 garlic cloves, minced
- 1 teaspoon dried oregano
- ♦ 2 cups frozen peas
- ♦ 3 plum tomatoes, chopped
- 1/4 cup chopped fresh parsley leaves
- 2 tablespoons red-wine vinegar
- 1 tablespoon olive oil
- 3/4 teaspoon salt
- 1/4 teaspoon black pepper

1 Combine wheat berries and water in medium saucepan over medium-high heat; bring to boil. Reduce heat to medium-low, cover, and simmer until berries are tender, about 1 hour. Drain and transfer to large bowl to cool.

2 Meanwhile, spray large nonstick skillet with nonstick spray and set over medium-high heat. Add bacon and cook until browned, 2–3 minutes per side. Transfer to paper towels to drain. Let cool; chop. Return skillet to medium heat and add onions, garlic, and oregano. Cook, stirring occasionally, until onions begin to brown, 5–6 minutes. Stir in peas and cook until bright green, 2–3 minutes longer. Remove from heat and let cool completely.

3 Add bacon, onion mixture, tomatoes, parsley, vinegar, oil, salt, and pepper to wheat berries and toss well. Serve at room temperature.

Per serving (1/2 cup): 143 Cal, 3 g Fat, 1 g Sat Fat, 0 g Trans Fat, 7 mg Chol, 351 mg Sod, 24 g Carb, 5 g Fib, 7 g Prot, 17 mg Calc. ***POINTS*** value: ***2.***

♦ FILLING EXTRA

Stir 3 grated carrots into this salad. This recipe works with the Simply Filling technique.

FROM TOP LEFT, CLOCKWISE: WATERMELON LEMONADE, PAGE 48; CORN ON THE COB WITH CHILI AND CILANTRO, PAGE 54; AND JAMAICAN JERK PORK TENDERLOIN WITH PINEAPPLE SALSA

Jamaican Jerk Pork Tenderloin with Pineapple Salsa

prep 20 MIN grill 30 MIN serves 12 level INTERMEDIATE

- ♦ 5 scallions, chopped
- 1/4 cup apple cider vinegar
- ♦ 1 Scotch bonnet or habanero pepper
- 4 garlic cloves
- 1 1/2 teaspoons ground allspice
- 1/4 teaspoon cinnamon
- 1/2 cup chopped fresh basil leaves
- 3 tablespoons + 2 teaspoons sugar
- 1 1/2 teaspoons salt
- ♦ 3 pounds pork tenderloins, trimmed
- ♦ 1 large pineapple, peeled, cored, and diced
- ♦ 1 small red onion, finely chopped
- ♦ 1 small red bell pepper, finely chopped
- 3 tablespoons lime juice

1 Combine scallions, vinegar, Scotch bonnet pepper, garlic, allspice, cinnamon, 1/4 cup basil, 3 tablespoons sugar, and 1 1/4 teaspoons salt in blender and puree. Transfer to zip-close plastic bag and add tenderloins. Squeeze out air and seal bag; turn to coat pork. Refrigerate, turning bag occasionally, at least 4 hours or up to 1 day.

2 Meanwhile, to make the salsa, combine pineapple, onion, bell pepper, lime juice, and remaining 1/4 cup basil, 2 teaspoons sugar, and 1/4 teaspoon salt in medium bowl. Cover and refrigerate.

3 Spray grill rack with nonstick spray; preheat grill to medium or prepare medium fire. Remove pork from marinade and place on grill rack; discard marinade. Cover grill and cook pork 15 minutes. Turn, cover, and cook until well marked and instant-read thermometer inserted into center of tenderloins registers 160°F, about 15 minutes longer. Let stand 10 minutes. Cut tenderloins into thin slices and serve with salsa.

Per serving (4 slices pork and 1/2 cup salsa): 190 Cal, 5 g Fat, 2 g Sat Fat, 0 g Trans Fat, 75 mg Chol, 345 mg Sod, 10 g Carb, 1 g Fib, 25 g Prot, 20 mg Calc. ***POINTS*** value: ***4.***

IN THE KITCHEN

If you can't find scorching-hot Scotch bonnet or habanero peppers at your grocer, substitute 2 jalapeño peppers. They won't have as much fiery heat, but they will still give you a nice zing. If you do use the hotter peppers, make sure you don't let the peppers themselves or the uncooked marinade touch your skin; the oils from these super-spicy peppers can burn your flesh.

Grilled Chicken with Balsamic Glaze

prep 10 MIN grill 20 MIN serves 12 level BASIC

- 1/2 cup ketchup
- 1/4 cup balsamic vinegar
- 1 teaspoon dried oregano
- 6 tablespoons packed light brown sugar
- 2 tablespoons paprika
- 1 tablespoon ground cumin
- 1 tablespoon chili powder
- 1 1/2 teaspoons salt
- 1 teaspoon black pepper
- ♦ 12 bone-in chicken drumsticks or thighs (about 3 1/2 pounds), trimmed

1 Spray grill rack with nonstick spray; preheat grill to medium or prepare medium fire.

2 For glaze, combine ketchup, vinegar, oregano, and 4 tablespoons brown sugar in small bowl. For spice rub, combine paprika, cumin, chili powder, salt, pepper, and remaining 2 tablespoons brown sugar in another small bowl. Rub spice rub under skin of chicken.

3 Place chicken on grill rack, cover grill, and grill 8 minutes. Turn, cover, and grill 8 minutes longer. Turn, brush chicken with half of glaze, and grill 3 minutes. Turn, brush chicken with remaining glaze, and grill until instant-read thermometer inserted into thickest part of chicken pieces without touching bone registers 165°F, about 3 minutes longer. Remove skin before eating.

Per serving (1 drumstick): 194 Cal, 8 g Fat, 2 g Sat Fat, 0 g Trans Fat, 67 mg Chol, 483 mg Sod, 11 g Carb, 1 g Fib, 19 g Prot, 27 mg Calc. ***POINTS*** value: ***4.***

♦ FILLING EXTRA

Serve with grilled onions: Cut 3 large red onions into thick slices and sprinkle the slices with paprika, cumin, chili powder, and salt. Grill them alongside the chicken until tender and browned.

GRILLED CHICKEN WITH BALSAMIC GLAZE AND MINTED GREEN BEAN SALAD, PAGE 55

Corn on the Cob with Chili and Cilantro

prep 10 MIN cook 10 MIN serves 12 level BASIC

- ♦ **8 ears sweet corn, each cut into thirds**
- **1 teaspoon chili powder**
- **1/2 teaspoon ground cumin**
- **1/4 teaspoon ancho chile powder**
- **1/4 teaspoon chipotle chile powder**
- **1 teaspoon salt**
- **2 tablespoons lime juice**
- **1 tablespoon olive oil**
- **2 tablespoons chopped fresh cilantro**

1 Bring large pot of lightly salted water to boil. Add corn; cover pot and boil corn 2 minutes.

2 Meanwhile, combine chili powder, cumin, ancho and chipotle chile powders, and salt in small bowl.

3 Drain corn, return it to pot, and add lime juice, oil, and cilantro; stir to coat. Sprinkle with spice mixture and stir again. Serve at once.

Per serving (2 pieces of corn): 64 Cal, 2 g Fat, 0 g Sat Fat, 0 g Trans Fat, 0 mg Chol, 206 mg Sod, 12 g Carb, 2 g Fib, 2 g Prot, 3 mg Calc. ***POINTS*** value: ***1.***

CHANGE IT UP

Give this recipe a Mediterranean flavor by substituting lemon juice for the lime juice and 1/4 cup chopped fresh basil and 1 tablespoon chopped fresh oregano for the cilantro and spices. The *POINTS* value for this variation will remain the same. This recipe works with the Simply Filling technique.

Minted Green Bean Salad

prep 20 MIN cook 10 MIN serves 12 level BASIC

- ♦ 2 pounds green beans, trimmed
- ♦ 1 pound plum tomatoes, chopped
- ♦ 1 large seedless cucumber, peeled, halved, and thinly sliced
- ♦ 1 red onion, thinly sliced
- ♦ 1 cup crumbled fat-free feta cheese
- 3 tablespoons chopped fresh mint leaves
- 1 tablespoon finely grated lemon zest
- 2 tablespoons lemon juice
- 1 tablespoon olive oil
- 3/4 teaspoon salt
- 1/4 teaspoon black pepper

Bring large pot of lightly salted water to boil. Add green beans; return to boil and cook 2 minutes. Drain beans, cool under cold running water, and drain again. Transfer to large bowl. Add tomatoes, cucumber, onion, feta, mint, lemon zest and juice, oil, salt, and pepper; toss well.

Per serving (1 cup): 62 Cal, 2 g Fat, 0 g Sat Fat, 0 g Trans Fat, 0 mg Chol, 303 mg Sod, 10 g Carb, 3 g Fib, 4 g Prot, 76 mg Calc. ***POINTS*** value: ***1.***

This recipe works with the Simply Filling technique.

Peach Crisp with Spiced Oat Topping

prep 15 MIN bake 45 MIN serves 12 level BASIC

- ♦ 3 (20-ounce) bags frozen unsweetened sliced peaches
- 2 teaspoons vanilla extract
- 1/4 teaspoon almond extract
- 1 cup sugar
- 1/2 cup + 2 tablespoons all-purpose flour
- 1/2 teaspoon ground ginger
- ♦ 1 cup old-fashioned oats
- 1/2 teaspoon cinnamon
- 1/4 teaspoon salt
- 1/4 cup unsalted butter, cut into small pieces
- 1 tablespoon water

1 Preheat oven to 375°F. Spray 3-quart baking dish with nonstick spray.

2 Combine peaches, vanilla extract, almond extract, 1/2 cup sugar, 2 tablespoons flour, and 1/4 teaspoon ginger in large bowl; mix well, transfer to baking dish and level top.

3 Combine oats, cinnamon, salt, and remaining 1/2 cup sugar, 1/2 cup flour, and 1/4 teaspoon ginger in medium bowl. Add butter and rub into mixture with your fingertips or cut it in with pastry cutter. Stir in water; with your hands, press mixture into clumps. Break clumps into smaller pieces and scatter over top of peach mixture. Bake until filling bubbles and top is golden, 45–50 minutes. Serve warm or at room temperature. To reheat, place in 300°F oven until heated through, 20–30 minutes.

Per serving (about 1 cup): 210 Cal, 4 g Fat, 2 g Sat Fat, 0 g Trans Fat, 10 mg Chol, 50 mg Sod, 39 g Carb, 3 g Fib, 3 g Prot, 7 mg Calc. ***POINTS*** value: ***4.***

CHANGE IT UP

To make a Peach-Cherry Crisp, substitute 1 (20-ounce) bag frozen unsweetened pitted cherries for 1 bag of the peaches, reduce the vanilla extract to 1 teaspoon, and up the flour in the filling mixture from 2 tablespoons to 3. The *POINTS* value will remain the same.

Hanukkah Buffet

POTATO AND CELERY ROOT LATKES WITH HORSERADISH SOUR CREAM AND HERB-CRUSTED ROAST SIDE OF SALMON, PAGE 61

Potato and Celery Root Latkes with Horseradish Sour Cream

prep 25 MIN cook 20 MIN serves 24 level INTERMEDIATE

- ♦ **1 cup fat-free sour cream**
- **2 tablespoons prepared horseradish in vinegar, drained**
- ♦ **2 pounds russet potatoes, peeled and shredded**
- ♦ **1 (1/2-pound) celery root, peeled and shredded**
- ♦ **1 small onion, peeled and shredded**
- ♦ **2 large eggs, lightly beaten**
- **1/4 cup all-purpose flour**
- **1 teaspoon salt**
- **1/4 teaspoon dried thyme**
- **1/4 teaspoon black pepper**
- **6 teaspoons canola oil**
- **Chopped chives**

1 Combine sour cream and horseradish in small bowl; cover and refrigerate.

2 Combine potatoes, celery root, onion, eggs, flour, salt, thyme, and pepper in large bowl; mix well. Form potato mixture into 24 disks, each about 2 1/2 inches in diameter.

3 Heat 2 teaspoons oil in large nonstick skillet over medium heat. Place 8 latkes in skillet and cook until browned and cooked through, 3–4 minutes per side; lower heat if latkes brown too quickly. Transfer to platter. Repeat with remaining oil and potato mixture. Sprinkle with chives and serve immediately with sour cream mixture. Latkes can also be made up to 1 day ahead, covered, refrigerated, and reheated on a baking sheet in 250°F oven until hot, 15–20 minutes.

Per serving (1 latke and 2 teaspoons sour cream): 68 Cal, 2 g Fat, 0 g Sat Fat, 0 g Trans Fat, 19 mg Chol, 124 mg Sod, 11 g Carb, 1 g Fib, 2 g Prot, 25 mg Calc. ***POINTS*** value: ***1.***

CHANGE IT UP

To make White and Sweet Potato Latkes, substitute 1/2 pound sweet potatoes, peeled and shredded, for the celery root. The *POINTS* value will remain the same.

Wild Mushroom Crostini

prep 20 MIN   bake/cook 15 MIN   serves 12   level INTERMEDIATE

Hanukkah Buffet
MENU FOR TWELVE

UP TO 2 WEEKS AHEAD
- ☐ Assemble Noodle Kugel but do not bake; wrap dish in foil and freeze.

3 DAYS AHEAD
- ☐ Make New York–Style Cheesecake with Pomegranate Syrup; refrigerate cake and syrup separately.

2 DAYS AHEAD
- ☐ Toast pita chips for Wild Mushroom Crostini; store in airtight container.
- ☐ Make Roast Vegetable Ratatouille; refrigerate.

1 DAY AHEAD
- ☐ Make horseradish sauce for Potato and Celery Root Latkes with Horseradish Sour Cream; make and refrigerate latkes if they are not to be cooked as guests arrive.
- ☐ Make topping for crostini; refrigerate.
- ☐ Thaw kugel in refrigerator.

2 HOURS AHEAD
- ☐ Bake kugel.

1 HOUR AHEAD
- ☐ Mix and form latkes if you're serving them fresh.
- ☐ Make Herb-Crusted Roast Side of Salmon; make Shepherd's Salad.
- ☐ Reheat topping and assemble crostini.

LAST MINUTE
- ☐ Reheat latkes if necessary, or begin cooking them as guests arrive.
- ☐ Reheat ratatouille, then transfer it to slow cooker set on low if you like.

6 multigrain pitas, each cut into 6 wedges
1 tablespoon olive oil
♦ **1 onion, chopped**
3 garlic cloves, minced
1/4 teaspoon dried oregano
♦ **1/4 pound shiitake mushrooms, stemmed and chopped**
♦ **1/4 pound oyster mushrooms, chopped**
♦ **1/4 pound cremini mushrooms, chopped**
1/4 teaspoon salt
1/4 teaspoon black pepper
1/4 pound light cream cheese (Neufchâtel), softened
1/4 cup grated Parmesan cheese
♦ **3 tablespoons fat-free milk**
2 tablespoons chopped fresh parsley leaves

1 Preheat oven to 425°F. Spray large baking sheet with nonstick spray.

2 Place pita wedges on baking sheet in single layer; bake until lightly browned and toasted, 6–7 minutes. Let cool. Wedges can be stored in airtight container up to 2 days.

3 Heat oil in large nonstick skillet over medium-high heat. Add onion, garlic, and oregano; cook, stirring, 2 minutes. Add all mushrooms, salt, and pepper; cook, stirring occasionally, until mushrooms are browned, 8–9 minutes. Remove from heat and stir in cream cheese, Parmesan, milk, and parsley. Top each pita wedge with 1 tablespoon mushroom mixture.

Per serving (3 crostini): 141 Cal, 5 g Fat, 2 g Sat Fat, 0 g Trans Fat, 9 mg Chol, 292 mg Sod, 21 g Carb, 3 g Fib, 6 g Prot, 50 mg Calc. ***POINTS*** value: ***3.***

Herb-Crusted Roast Side of Salmon

prep 15 MIN roast 30 MIN serves 12 level BASIC

- **2 slices whole wheat bread, crusts removed**
- **1/2 cup chopped fresh parsley leaves**
- **1/3 cup chopped fresh dill**
- **1 tablespoon finely grated lemon zest**
- ♦ **3 pounds salmon fillet (preferably in one piece), skin on, pinbones removed**
- **3/4 teaspoon salt**
- **1/4 teaspoon black pepper**
- **3 tablespoons Dijon mustard**

1 Preheat oven to 450°F. Spray large baking sheet with nonstick spray.

2 Put bread in food processor and pulse to make coarse crumbs. Transfer to medium bowl and stir in parsley, dill, and lemon zest.

3 Sprinkle flesh side of salmon with salt and pepper and spread evenly with mustard. Sprinkle bread crumb mixture over mustard, pressing lightly to help it adhere. Place salmon, skin side down, on prepared baking sheet. Cover loosely with foil and roast in center of oven 20–25 minutes or until fish is almost cooked through. Remove foil and roast 3–4 minutes longer or until fish flakes easily with fork. Cut into 12 slices and serve hot or at room temperature.

Per serving (1 slice): 148 Cal, 4 g Fat, 1 g Sat Fat, 0 g Trans Fat, 59 mg Chol, 341 mg Sod, 3 g Carb, 1 g Fib, 23 g Prot, 28 mg Calc. ***POINTS*** value: ***3.***

IN THE KITCHEN

This salmon is moist and flavorful on its own, but if you'd like to serve it with a lemon sauce, simply combine 1/2 cup light mayonnaise with lemon juice to taste and 1–2 pinches of cayenne. Each 2-teaspoon serving has a *POINTS* value of *1.*

Noodle Kugel

prep 15 MIN   cook/bake 55 MIN   serves 12   level BASIC

- 3/4 pound wide yolkless noodles
- ♦ 5 large eggs, lightly beaten
- ♦ 1 (16-ounce) container fat-free cottage cheese
- ♦ 1 cup fat-free milk
- 1/4 cup reduced-fat sour cream
- 1/2 cup pitted dates, sliced
- 1/2 cup dried apricots, sliced
- 1/4 teaspoon ground nutmeg
- 1/4 teaspoon salt
- 8 tablespoons sugar
- 2 cups cornflakes, crushed
- 2 tablespoons unsalted butter, melted

1 Preheat oven to 350°F. Spray 3-quart baking dish with nonstick spray.

2 Cook noodles according to package directions, omitting salt if desired; drain well.

3 Meanwhile, combine eggs, cottage cheese, milk, sour cream, dates, apricots, nutmeg, salt, and 6 tablespoons sugar in large bowl and whisk until combined. Add noodles and toss well. Transfer to prepared baking dish. Stir remaining 2 tablespoons sugar, cornflakes, and melted butter together in small bowl; sprinkle over top of noodle mixture. Bake until edges are lightly browned and knife inserted into center comes out clean, 35–40 minutes. Let stand 10 minutes; cut into 12 squares. Serve warm or at room temperature.

Per serving (1 square): 272 Cal, 5 g Fat, 2 g Sat Fat, 0 g Trans Fat, 98 mg Chol, 270 mg Sod, 45 g Carb, 2 g Fib, 12 g Prot, 76 mg Calc. ***POINTS*** value: **5.**

Shepherd's Salad

prep 20 MIN cook NONE serves 12 level BASIC

- ♦ 3 pints grape tomatoes, halved
- ♦ 2 seedless cucumbers, peeled and chopped
- ♦ 2 large green bell peppers, chopped
- ♦ 1 small red onion, chopped
- 1/2 cup chopped fresh parsley leaves
- 3 tablespoons chopped fresh mint leaves
- 2 tablespoons red-wine vinegar
- 2 tablespoons olive oil
- 1/2 teaspoon salt
- 1/4 teaspoon black pepper
- ♦ 1 cup crumbled fat-free feta cheese

Combine tomatoes, cucumbers, bell peppers, onion, parsley, mint, vinegar, oil, salt, and black pepper in large bowl and toss to combine. Add feta and toss again.

Per serving (1 cup): 74 Cal, 3 g Fat, 1 g Sat Fat, 0 g Trans Fat, 3 mg Chol, 223 mg Sod, 8 g Carb, 2 g Fib, 4 g Prot, 27 mg Calc. ***POINTS*** value: ***1.***

FILLING EXTRA

If you have leftovers or just want to make this delicious salad a stand-alone meal, toss each serving with 1/3 cup cooked whole wheat couscous and 1 chopped cooked skinless, boneless chicken breast (3 ounces cooked weight). Each serving will increase in *POINTS* value by *4.* This recipe works with the Simply Filling technique.

Roast Vegetable Ratatouille

prep 30 MIN roast/cook 1 HR 5 MIN serves 12 level BASIC

- ♦ **3 pounds eggplant, cut into 1/2-inch cubes**
- **3 tablespoons olive oil**
- ♦ **2 pounds zucchini, cut into 1/2-inch cubes**
- ♦ **3 onions, chopped**
- ♦ **2 red bell peppers, cut into 1/2-inch pieces**
- **2 shallots, chopped**
- **6 garlic cloves, minced**
- **1 teaspoon dried basil**
- ♦ **2 (14 1/2-ounce) cans diced tomatoes**
- **1/2 teaspoon salt**
- **1/4 teaspoon black pepper**

1 Place oven racks in upper third and lower third of oven. Preheat oven to 450°F. Spray 2 large baking sheets with nonstick spray.

2 Combine eggplant in large bowl with 2 tablespoons oil; toss well. Spread eggplant on prepared baking sheets and roast, tossing occasionally and rotating baking sheets top to bottom once, until tender and lightly browned, about 30 minutes. Transfer to large bowl.

3 Toss zucchini, onions, and bell peppers in another bowl with remaining 1 tablespoon oil. Spray baking sheets again with nonstick spray and spread mixture evenly on them. Roast, tossing occasionally and rotating baking sheets top to bottom once, until vegetables are tender and lightly browned, about 30 minutes. Transfer to bowl with eggplant.

4 Meanwhile, spray large nonstick skillet or nonstick Dutch oven with nonstick spray and set over medium-high heat. Add shallots, garlic, and basil; cook, stirring, 2 minutes. Stir in tomatoes; cook, stirring occasionally, until mixture begins to thicken, 8–9 minutes. Stir in eggplant mixture, salt, and pepper; cook until heated through.

Per serving (3/4 cup): 113 Cal, 4 g Fat, 1 g Sat Fat, 0 g Trans Fat, 0 mg Chol, 191 mg Sod, 19 g Carb, 6 g Fib, 3 g Prot, 43 mg Calc. ***POINTS*** value: ***2.***

This recipe works with the Simply Filling technique.

New York–Style Cheesecake with Pomegranate Syrup

prep 20 MIN bake/cook 1 HR 10 MIN serves 16 level INTERMEDIATE

- **12 low-fat graham crackers**
- **1 cup + 8 tablespoons sugar**
- **2 tablespoons unsalted butter, melted**
- **1 (8-ounce) package light cream cheese (Neufchâtel)**
- **1 (8-ounce) package fat-free cream cheese**
- ♦ **1 (16-ounce) container fat-free sour cream**
- ♦ **2 large eggs**
- ♦ **2 large egg whites**
- **1 teaspoon vanilla extract**
- **2 cups pomegranate juice**

1 Preheat oven to 350°F. Spray bottom and sides of 9-inch springform pan lightly with nonstick spray.

2 Combine graham crackers and 2 tablespoons sugar in food processor; pulse to make fine crumbs. Transfer to small bowl and stir in melted butter. Press crumb mixture evenly onto bottom and halfway up sides of springform pan. Bake until golden, 8–10 minutes; cool completely on rack.

3 Combine light cream cheese, fat-free cream cheese, and sour cream in large bowl; beat with electric mixer on medium speed until smooth. Add eggs, egg whites, vanilla, and 1 cup sugar; beat just until combined, stopping once or twice to scrape down sides of bowl. Pour mixture over crust in pan and transfer to oven. Reduce oven temperature to 325°F. Bake until cake is set around edges but still jiggles slightly in center when shaken, about 1 hour. Turn off oven and let cake sit in oven 1 hour longer. Refrigerate until chilled, at least 3 hours.

4 Meanwhile, combine remaining 6 tablespoons sugar and pomegranate juice in small saucepan; bring to boil over medium-high heat. Reduce heat to medium and simmer until liquid is thick enough to coat back of spoon, about 30 minutes. Transfer to small bowl and refrigerate until chilled.

5 Remove cheesecake from springform pan and place on platter. Pour half of pomegranate syrup over top. Cut cake into 16 slices. Spoon small amount of remaining syrup over each slice.

Per serving (1 slice cheesecake and 2 teaspoons syrup): 215 Cal, 6 g Fat, 4 g Sat Fat, 0 g Trans Fat, 45 mg Chol, 192 mg Sod, 34 g Carb, 0 g Fib, 6 g Prot, 83 mg Calc. ***POINTS*** value: **5.**

Girls' Night In Dinner Party

Raspberry-Champagne Cocktails

prep 5 MIN cook NONE serves 4 level BASIC

- **3/4 cup raspberry-cranberry juice**
- **1 1/2 cups sparkling white wine, chilled**
- **1 cup lemon-lime seltzer, chilled**
- **Ice cubes**
- ♦ **1/2 cup fresh raspberries**
- **4 small mint sprigs**

Combine juice, wine, and seltzer in pitcher. Fill 4 wine glasses with ice; divide cocktail mixture evenly among glasses. Garnish each glass with raspberries and a mint sprig.

Per serving (1 glass): 99 cal, 0 g Fat, 0 g Sat Fat, 0 g Trans Fat, 0 mg Chol, 5 mg Sod, 10 g Carb, 1 g Fib, 0 g Prot, 15 mg Calc. ***POINTS*** value: **2.**

Girls' Night In Dinner Party

MENU FOR FOUR

2 DAYS AHEAD

- ☐ Make Chocolate-Pecan Cookies.

1 DAY AHEAD

- ☐ Make Ricotta Cream Custards with Raspberry Sauce; refrigerate custards and sauce separately.
- ☐ Make Barley Pilaf with Peas; refrigerate.
- ☐ Chill wine and seltzer for Raspberry-Champagne Cocktails.

1 HOUR AHEAD

- ☐ Prepare Peach-Glazed Cornish Hens.
- ☐ Make Coconut Shrimp; serve as an hors d'oeuvre while hens finish roasting.

LAST MINUTE

- ☐ Make cocktails.
- ☐ Reheat pilaf; serve with hens.

Coconut Shrimp

prep 25 MIN bake 10 MIN serves 4 level BASIC

- **6 tablespoons flaked unsweetened coconut**
- **1/4 cup panko (Japanese bread crumbs)**
- **2 tablespoons all-purpose flour**
- **1/2 teaspoon salt**
- ♦ **4 large egg whites**
- ♦ **24 medium shrimp (about 1/2 pound), peeled with tails left on, deveined, butterflied, and patted dry**

1 Preheat oven to 450°F. Spray baking sheet with nonstick spray.

2 Combine coconut, panko, flour, and salt on piece of wax paper. Beat egg whites in large bowl until frothy; add shrimp to egg whites and toss to coat. Lift shrimp from egg whites one at a time, letting excess drip back into bowl; coat with coconut mixture, pressing gently to help it adhere. Place shrimp in single layer on baking sheet. Spray shrimp lightly with nonstick spray. Bake until golden outside and opaque inside, 8–10 minutes.

Per serving (6 shrimp): 128 Cal, 4 g Fat, 3 g Sat Fat, 0 g Trans Fat, 84 mg Chol, 450 mg Sod, 9 g Carb, 1 g Fib, 14 g Prot, 22 mg Calc. ***POINTS*** value: ***3.***

♦ FILLING EXTRA

Serve these crispy shrimp with a quick pineapple salsa made with 2 cups drained and diced unsweetened canned pineapple, 1 small seeded and chopped jalapeño pepper, and 1/4 cup chopped fresh cilantro; a 1/2 cup of salsa per person will increase the per-serving *POINTS* value by *1.*

COCONUT SHRIMP AND RASPBERRY-CHAMPAGNE COCKTAILS, PAGE 67

Peach-Glazed Cornish Hens

prep 25 MIN roast/cook 1 HOUR 5 MIN serves 4 level INTERMEDIATE

- **2 tablespoons Dijon mustard**
- **2 garlic cloves, minced**
- **1/8 teaspoon salt**
- **1/4 cup + 2 teaspoons peach preserves**
- ♦ **2 (1-pound) Cornish game hens**
- ♦ **1 cup reduced-sodium chicken broth**
- **2 shallots, minced**
- **2 teaspoons chopped fresh thyme leaves**
- **2 teaspoons unsalted butter**

1 Preheat oven to 450°F.

2 Combine mustard, garlic, salt, and 1/4 cup preserves in small bowl. Gently loosen skin from breasts of hens; spoon preserve mixture evenly under skin. Secure legs of each hen with kitchen twine and tuck wing tips under hens. Place hens in shallow roasting pan and roast, uncovered, until instant-read thermometer inserted into thickest part of thighs without touching bone registers 180°F, about 1 hour.

3 Transfer hens to platter; cover loosely with foil and keep warm. Set roasting pan directly over two burners turned to high heat. Add broth, shallots, thyme, and remaining 2 teaspoons preserves; bring to boil, scraping any browned bits from bottom of pan. Reduce heat and simmer until sauce is reduced to about 1/2 cup, 4–5 minutes. Remove from heat; swirl in butter. Remove and discard skin from hens; split each in half down breastbone, cut around backbone, and place one half hen on each plate. Serve with sauce.

Per serving (1/2 hen and 2 tablespoons sauce): 228 Cal, 6 g Fat, 2 g Sat Fat, 0 g Trans Fat, 103 mg Chol, 412 mg Sod, 19 g Carb, 1 g Fib, 23 g Prot, 36 mg Calc. ***POINTS*** value: ***5.***

Barley Pilaf with Peas

prep 5 MIN cook 35 MIN serves 4 level BASIC

- 2 cups water
- ♦ 1/2 cup barley
- 1 1/2 teaspoons olive oil
- ♦ 1 small onion, thinly sliced
- 2 garlic cloves, minced
- ♦ 1 cup frozen peas, thawed
- 1 tablespoon grated lemon zest
- 1/2 teaspoon salt

1 Bring water to boil in small saucepan. Add barley and return to boil. Reduce heat and simmer, covered, until barley is tender, 30–35 minutes; drain.

2 Meanwhile, heat oil in large nonstick saucepan over medium-high heat. Add onion and cook, stirring occasionally, until softened, 6–8 minutes. Stir in garlic; cook 1 minute. Add cooked barley, peas, lemon zest, and salt. Cook, stirring occasionally, until peas are heated through, 3–4 minutes.

Per serving (3/4 cup): 154 Cal, 4 g Fat, 1 g Sat Fat, 0 g Trans Fat, 0 mg Chol, 329 mg Sod, 25 g Carb, 7 g Fib, 5 g Prot, 28 mg Calc. ***POINTS*** value: ***3.***

CHANGE IT UP

Want a super-speedy version of this whole-grain dish? Just substitute 1/2 cup whole wheat couscous for the barley, preparing it according to package directions. The whole dish can be on the table in about 15 minutes, and the *POINTS* value will remain the same. This recipe works with the Simply Filling technique.

Ricotta Cream Custards with Raspberry Sauce

prep 15 MIN cook NONE serves 4 level INTERMEDIATE

- **6 ounces fat-free cream cheese**
- ♦ **1 cup fat-free ricotta cheese**
- **1 1/2 teaspoons vanilla extract**
- **8 tablespoons confectioners' sugar**
- ♦ **1/2 cup fat-free Greek yogurt**
- **1/4 cup thawed frozen fat-free whipped topping**
- ♦ **1/2 cup fresh or frozen unsweetened raspberries, thawed**
- **2 tablespoons seedless raspberry jam**

1 Beat cream cheese with electric mixer on high speed in medium bowl until smooth. Beat in ricotta, vanilla, and 6 tablespoons confectioners' sugar. Gently fold in yogurt and whipped topping with rubber spatula.

2 Cut out 4 (8-inch) squares cheesecloth; dampen slightly with cold water. Line 4 (6-ounce) ramekins or custard cups with cheesecloth, allowing excess to hang over edges. Spoon cream cheese mixture into ramekins. Fold excess cheesecloth over tops. Refrigerate until set, about 4 hours or overnight.

3 Meanwhile, combine raspberries, jam, and remaining 2 tablespoons confectioners' sugar in food processor and puree. Pour mixture through sieve set over bowl, pressing on solids with spoon to extract as much liquid as possible; discard solids. Cover sauce and refrigerate.

4 Pour off any liquid that has collected inside molds. Invert molds on dessert plates; peel off cheesecloth. Spoon or drizzle sauce around plates.

Per serving (1 custard with 2 tablespoons sauce): 208 Cal, 1 g Fat, 0 g Sat Fat, 0 g Trans Fat, 13 mg Chol, 310 mg Sod, 33 g Carb, 1 g Fib, 14 g Prot, 201 mg Calc. ***POINTS*** value: ***4.***

IN THE KITCHEN

This recipe is based on the French classic *coeur à la crème* ("heart of cream"), a dessert traditionally made in heart-shaped porcelain molds and a favorite for serving on Valentine's Day. Look for the molds online or in kitchenware stores if you'd like to give this delicious dessert a romantic touch.

Chocolate-Pecan Cookies

prep 20 MIN cook 15 MIN serves 24 level INTERMEDIATE

- **2 1/3 cups confectioners' sugar**
- **3/4 cup Dutch-process cocoa powder**
- **1/8 teaspoon salt**
- ♦ **3 large egg whites, at room temperature**
- **2 teaspoons chocolate extract**
- **1 cup pecans, chopped**

1 Place oven racks in upper and lower thirds of oven; preheat oven to 350°F. Line 2 large baking sheets with parchment paper.

2 Sift confectioners' sugar, cocoa, and salt into medium bowl. With electric mixer on low speed, beat egg whites into cocoa mixture until blended. Increase speed to high and continue beating 1 minute. Beat in chocolate extract. Fold in pecans.

3 Drop dough by level tablespoonfuls onto baking sheets, making 24 cookies and leaving 2 inches between them. Bake until shiny, cracked, and firm to the touch, 13–15 minutes. Cool on baking sheets. Store in airtight container up to 3 days.

Per serving (1 cookie): 82 Cal, 3 g Fat, 0 g Sat Fat, 0 g Trans Fat, 0 mg Chol, 20 mg Sod, 14 g Carb, 1 g Fib, 2 g Prot, 8 mg Calc. ***POINTS*** value: ***2.***

IN THE KITCHEN

Want to send your guests home with a tasty gift? Stack three of these cookies on top of each other, then wrap in plastic wrap or clear cellophane gift wrap, bunching the wrap at the top and tying it off with a pretty ribbon.

Time With Family

CHAPTER 2

Chinese New Year

Hot-and-Sour Soup

prep 25 MIN cook 20 MIN serves 6 level BASIC

- ♦ **2 (14½-ounce) cans reduced-sodium chicken broth**
- **¾ cup cold water**
- ♦ **2 heads baby bok choy, stems thinly sliced, leaves chopped**
- ♦ **¼ pound shiitake mushrooms, stems discarded, caps thinly sliced**
- ♦ **1 red bell pepper, chopped**
- **3 tablespoons apple cider vinegar**
- **1 tablespoon reduced-sodium soy sauce**
- **2 teaspoons Asian chili-and-garlic paste**
- ♦ **3 ounces low-sodium lean ham, diced**
- **1 tablespoon cornstarch**
- ♦ **3 scallions, thinly sliced**
- **1½ teaspoons sesame oil**
- **½ teaspoon black pepper**

1 Bring broth and ½ cup water to boil in large saucepan over high heat. Stir in bok choy stems, mushrooms, bell pepper, vinegar, soy sauce, and chili-and-garlic paste. Return to boil; reduce heat and simmer 5 minutes. Stir in bok choy leaves and ham; simmer 3 minutes longer.

2 Stir remaining ¼ cup water and cornstarch together in small cup until smooth, then stir mixture into soup. Cook, stirring, until soup thickens slightly, about 1 minute. Stir in scallions, sesame oil, and pepper. Ladle into 6 soup bowls.

Per serving (1 cup): 80 Cal, 2 g Fat, 1 g Sat Fat, 0 g Trans Fat, 9 mg Chol, 417 mg Sod, 9 g Carb, 2 g Fib, 6 g Prot, 78 mg Calc. ***POINTS*** value: ***1.***

CHANGE IT UP

For vegetarian hot-and-sour soup, replace the chicken broth with vegetable broth, use baked tofu (preferably teriyaki flavor) instead of lean ham, and add ½ cup drained canned chopped bamboo shoots along with the mushrooms. The *POINTS* value will remain the same.

Chinese New Year

MENU FOR SIX

UP TO 2 DAYS AHEAD

- ☐ Roast fruit for Roast Pineapple and Strawberries with Mango Sorbet; refrigerate.

1 DAY AHEAD

- ☐ Make Hot-and-Sour Soup; let cool and refrigerate.
- ☐ Make Shrimp Dumplings; let cool and refrigerate.

EARLY IN THE DAY

- ☐ Assemble and prepare all ingredients for Orange Beef and Broccoli; cover and refrigerate perishable ingredients.
- ☐ Assemble and prepare all ingredients for Seven-Vegetable Stir-Fry with Noodles; cover and refrigerate perishable ingredients.

30 MINUTES AHEAD

- ☐ Make seven-vegetable stir-fry.

LAST MINUTE

- ☐ Make orange beef.
- ☐ Reheat soup and dumplings.
- ☐ Bring roast pineapple and strawberries to room temperature before serving dessert.

Shrimp Dumplings

prep 30 MIN cook/steam 30 MIN serves 6 level ADVANCED

- ♦ 2 **cups coleslaw mix**
- ♦ 2 **scallions, cut into 1-inch pieces**
- 3/4 **cup lightly packed fresh cilantro leaves**
- ♦ 1/2 **pound medium shrimp, peeled and deveined**
- ♦ 1 **large egg white**
- 1 **teaspoon sesame oil**
- 24 **wonton skins**
- 2 **tablespoons reduced-sodium soy sauce**
- 2 **tablespoons unseasoned rice vinegar**
- 1/2 **teaspoon hot pepper sauce**

1 Bring medium saucepan two thirds full of water to boil over high heat. Add coleslaw mix and cook until wilted, about 30 seconds. Drain, rinse under cold running water, and drain again. Pat dry with paper towels.

2 Put scallions and cilantro in food processor; pulse until finely chopped. Add shrimp and coleslaw mix and continue to pulse until finely chopped. Add egg white and sesame oil and pulse until blended.

3 Cut circles from wonton skins with 3-inch round cookie cutter. Lay circles on work surface and spoon 1 level tablespoon of shrimp mixture into center of each. Gather up edges, pleating wonton skins around filling but leaving filling uncovered at top. Press down lightly on filling with moistened finger so that dumplings resemble small flowers.

4 Fill large, deep skillet with 1 inch water. Set steamer basket in skillet and spray basket with nonstick spray. Arrange half of dumplings in basket. Set skillet over high heat and bring to boil; reduce heat to medium, cover skillet tightly, and steam dumplings until filling is firm and cooked through, about 10 minutes. Transfer dumplings to platter and cover to keep warm. Repeat with remaining dumplings.

5 Meanwhile, stir soy sauce, rice vinegar, and hot sauce together in small bowl. Serve dumplings with sauce.

Per serving (4 dumplings and 2 teaspoons sauce): 142 Cal, 2 g Fat, 0 g Sat Fat, 0 g Trans Fat, 59 mg Chol, 476 mg Sod, 20 g Carb, 1 g Fib, 10 g Prot, 40 mg Calc. ***POINTS*** value: ***3.***

MAKE AHEAD

You can make and steam the dumplings 1 day ahead. To reheat, steam them again just before serving until they are heated through, about 3 minutes.

Orange Beef and Broccoli

prep 25 MIN cook 10 MIN serves 6 level INTERMEDIATE

- ♦ 1 large bunch broccoli
- ♦ 4 navel oranges
- 1 tablespoon cornstarch
- 1/4 teaspoon red pepper flakes
- 3 tablespoons reduced-sodium soy sauce
- ♦ 1 (1 1/4-pound) flank steak, trimmed, halved lengthwise, and thinly sliced crosswise
- 1/3 cup water
- ♦ 1 red bell pepper, thinly sliced
- ♦ 3 scallions, cut into 1-inch pieces
- 3 large garlic cloves, minced
- 1 tablespoon minced peeled fresh ginger

1 Remove florets from stems of broccoli and cut into bite-size pieces. Trim, peel, and thinly slice stems.

2 Grate 1 teaspoon orange zest from 1 orange, then squeeze 3/4 cup juice (from about 2 oranges) into measuring cup. Stir in cornstarch, pepper flakes, orange zest, and 2 tablespoons soy sauce. Remove peel and white pith from remaining oranges and cut into segments.

3 Spray nonstick wok or large deep nonstick skillet with nonstick spray and set over medium-high heat. Toss beef with remaining 1 tablespoon soy sauce in large bowl. Add half of beef to wok; stir-fry just until beef is no longer pink, about 1 minute. Transfer to plate. Repeat with remaining beef.

4 Add broccoli florets and stems and water to wok. Cover and cook 1 minute. Uncover, add bell pepper, and stir-fry 1 minute. Stir in scallions, garlic, and ginger; stir-fry until fragrant, about 1 minute. Stir orange juice mixture and add to wok. Stir-fry until sauce thickens, about 1 minute. Stir in beef and cook until heated thoroughly through. Spoon mixture onto platter and top with orange segments.

Per serving (about 1 2/3 cups): 244 Cal, 9 g Fat, 5 g Sat Fat, 0 g Trans Fat, 48 mg Chol, 820 mg Sod, 19 g Carb, 5 g Fib, 23 g Prot, 87 mg Calc. ***POINTS*** value: ***5.***

♦ FILLING EXTRA

Serve over 1/2 cup cooked brown rice; this will increase the per-serving *POINTS* value by *2.*

Seven-Vegetable Stir-Fry with Noodles

prep 25 MIN cook 20 MIN serves 6 level BASIC

- ♦ 6 ounces whole wheat linguine
- 3/4 cup water
- 1/4 cup hoisin sauce
- 2 teaspoons cornstarch
- ♦ 3 carrots, thinly sliced on the diagonal
- ♦ 1 red onion, halved and sliced
- ♦ 1/4 pound shiitake mushrooms, stems discarded, caps quartered
- ♦ 1 pound asparagus, cut into 1 1/2-inch pieces
- 1 tablespoon minced peeled fresh ginger
- 4 garlic cloves, minced
- ♦ 1/4 pound snow peas, trimmed and halved
- ♦ 1/4 pound snap peas, trimmed and stringed
- ♦ 1 (15-ounce) can baby corn, drained, rinsed, and halved
- 2 tablespoons unseasoned rice vinegar
- 2 teaspoons sesame oil

1 Cook linguine according to package directions, omitting salt if desired. Drain and keep warm.

2 Meanwhile, stir water, hoisin sauce, and cornstarch in small bowl until smooth.

3 Spray nonstick wok or large deep nonstick skillet with nonstick spray and set over medium-high heat. Add carrots and stir-fry 1 minute. Add onion and mushrooms and stir-fry until tender, 2–3 minutes. Add asparagus and stir-fry 1 minute. Add ginger and garlic and stir-fry 30 seconds. Stir hoisin mixture and add to wok along with snow peas, snap peas, and corn. Cook until sauce simmers and thickens, about 2 minutes.

4 Remove wok from heat and stir in vinegar and oil. Transfer linguine to platter and top with vegetable mixture.

Per serving (1 1/3 cups vegetables and 1/2 cup linguine): 215 Cal, 3 g Fat, 0 g Sat Fat, 0 g Trans Fat, 0 mg Chol, 298 mg Sod, 43 g Carb, 8 g Fib, 8 g Prot, 56 mg Calc. ***POINTS*** value: ***4.***

SEVEN-VEGETABLE STIR-FRY WITH NOODLES

Roast Pineapple and Strawberries with Mango Sorbet

prep 15 MIN roast 15 MIN serves 6 level BASIC

- 3 tablespoons packed light brown sugar
- 1/2 teaspoon five-spice powder
- ♦ 1 small ripe pineapple, peeled, cored, and cut into 3/4-inch chunks
- ♦ 1 (1-pound) container strawberries, hulled and halved
- 1 pint mango sorbet
- 6 store-bought fortune cookies

1 Preheat oven to 425°F. Spray 15 x 10-inch jelly-roll pan with nonstick spray.

2 Stir brown sugar and five-spice powder together in small bowl. Spread pineapple chunks on pan and sprinkle with brown sugar mixture. Roast, stirring once halfway through cooking time, until pineapple softens and browns in a few spots, about 10 minutes. Add strawberries to pan; roast until strawberries are slightly softened and begin to release some juice, about 5 minutes. Let cool.

3 Spoon fruit mixture into 6 dessert dishes. Top each with 1/3-cup scoop mango sorbet. Serve with fortune cookies.

Per serving (3/4 cup fruit, 1/3 cup sorbet, 1 fortune cookie): 177 Cal, 1 g Fat, 0 g Sat Fat, 0 g Trans Fat, 0 mg Chol, 26 mg Sod, 44 g Carb, 3 g Fib, 1 g Prot, 21 mg Calc. ***POINTS*** value: ***3.***

IN THE KITCHEN

Peeled and cored pineapples are usually available in grocery stores; purchase one and you can knock a few minutes off your prep time.

Passover Dinner

CHICKEN SOUP WITH PARSLEY MATZO BALLS

Chicken Soup with Parsley Matzo Balls

prep 30 MIN cook 1 HR 30 MIN serves 12 level INTERMEDIATE

- ♦ **12 cups reduced-sodium fat-free chicken broth**
- ♦ **1 (3-pound) chicken, cut into 8 pieces, skin and wings removed and discarded**
- ♦ **4 carrots, sliced**
- ♦ **2 parsnips, sliced**
- **5 sprigs fresh parsley**
- **4 sprigs fresh dill**
- **1 1/4 cups matzo meal**
- ♦ **3 large eggs, lightly beaten**
- ♦ **2 large egg whites**
- **1 tablespoon olive oil**
- **3/4 teaspoon salt**
- **1/4 teaspoon black pepper**
- **1/3 cup + 1 tablespoon chopped fresh parsley leaves**

1 To make soup, combine broth, chicken pieces, carrots, parsnips, parsley sprigs, and dill in large pot over medium-high heat; bring to boil. Reduce heat, cover, and simmer until chicken and vegetables are tender, about 1 hour.

2 Meanwhile, to make matzo balls, combine matzo meal, eggs, egg whites, oil, salt, pepper, and 1/3 cup chopped parsley in medium bowl. Refrigerate 30 minutes. Form into 24 balls.

3 Remove chicken pieces from broth; reserve for another use. Remove and discard parsley sprigs and dill sprigs. Return broth to simmer and add matzo balls; simmer, covered, until matzo balls are cooked through, 20–25 minutes. Sprinkle with remaining 1 tablespoon chopped parsley.

Per serving (1 cup soup and 2 matzo balls): 206 Cal, 7 g Fat, 2 g Sat Fat, 0 g Trans Fat, 94 mg Chol, 326 mg Sod, 17 g Carb, 2 g Fib, 19 g Prot, 49 mg Calc. ***POINTS*** value: ***4.***

IN THE KITCHEN

Poaching a whole chicken in broth gives this soup an incredibly rich flavor. Pull the meat from the bones and use in salads, sandwiches, tacos, or chili.

Homemade Gefilte Fish

Passover Dinner

MENU FOR TWELVE

3 DAYS AHEAD
- ☐ Bake Coconut Macaroons.

2 DAYS AHEAD
- ☐ Make Tomato and Garlic–Braised Brisket; cool and refrigerate in pot.
- ☐ Prepare Homemade Gefilte Fish.
- ☐ Make soup for Chicken Soup with Parsley Matzo Balls; refrigerate.

1 DAY AHEAD
- ☐ Prepare Pear and Apple Haroset.
- ☐ Cook and cool haricots verts for Lemon-Dijon Haricots Verts, wrap in paper towels and plastic; refrigerate.

EARLY IN THE DAY
- ☐ Make and poach matzo balls; remove from soup and store separately.
- ☐ Bake Matzo Farfel with Asparagus and Mushrooms; refrigerate.

1 HOUR AHEAD
- ☐ Make lemon-Dijon dressing for haricots verts; refrigerate.

30 MINUTES AHEAD
- ☐ Reheat matzo farfel in 300°F oven about 25 minutes.

LAST MINUTE
- ☐ Reheat soup; add matzo balls.
- ☐ Reheat brisket.
- ☐ Toss haricots with dressing.

prep 25 MIN cook 1 HR 15 MIN serves 12 level INTERMEDIATE

- ♦ **3 carrots, sliced**
- ♦ **2 small onions, sliced**
- ♦ **1 pound skinless cod fillet, cut into chunks**
- ♦ **1 pound skinless flounder fillet, cut into chunks**
- ♦ **2 large eggs**
- **1/4 cup matzo meal**
- **3/4 teaspoon salt**
- **1/4 teaspoon black pepper**
- ♦ **8 cups low-sodium fish broth**
- ♦ **1 parsnip, peeled and sliced**
- **4 cups water**
- **1/4 cup prepared horseradish in vinegar, drained**

1 Combine 1 carrot and 1 onion in food processor and pulse until chopped. Add cod, flounder, eggs, matzo meal, salt, and pepper; pulse until mixture is fairly smooth. Transfer to medium bowl, cover, and refrigerate.

2 Combine broth, parsnip, water, remaining 2 carrots, and remaining onion in large pot. Bring to boil over high heat. Reduce heat, cover, and simmer 20 minutes.

3 With damp hands, form fish mixture into 12 ovals, using about 1/3 cup for each. Increase heat to medium high and drop ovals into broth mixture; return to simmer. Cover, reduce heat to medium low, and simmer until gefilte fish is cooked through, 50–55 minutes. Remove from heat and cool in pot.

4 Transfer gefilte fish and vegetables to large plastic container and spoon in enough broth to cover; reserve remaining broth for another use. Chill gefilte fish and vegetables at least 2 hours or up to 2 days. With slotted spoon, transfer to platter; serve with horseradish.

Per serving (1 piece gefilte fish, 1/4 cup vegetables, and 1 teaspoon horseradish): 131 Cal, 3 g Fat, 1 g Sat Fat, 0 g Trans Fat, 71 mg Chol, 309 mg Sod, 9 g Carb, 2 g Fib, 18 g Prot, 38 mg Calc. ***POINTS*** value: **2.**

MAKE AHEAD

The flavor of this delicate dish deepens and improves as the dumplings sit in the poaching liquid, so make it a day or two ahead if you can.

Tomato and Garlic–Braised Brisket

prep 10 MIN cook 4 HRS 15 MIN serves 12 level BASIC

- **2 teaspoons olive oil**
- **4 pounds center-cut brisket, trimmed**
- **1 teaspoon ground cumin**
- **1 teaspoon salt**
- **1/4 teaspoon black pepper**
- ♦ **1 onion, chopped**
- **1/2 cup red wine or reduced-sodium beef broth**
- **4 garlic cloves, minced**
- **1 teaspoon dried oregano**
- ♦ **1 (28-ounce) can diced tomatoes**

1 Heat oil in nonstick Dutch oven over medium-high heat. Sprinkle brisket all over with cumin, salt, and pepper; add to Dutch oven and cook until browned, about 4 minutes per side. Transfer to plate and set aside.

2 Return Dutch oven to stove and add onion, wine, garlic, and oregano; bring to boil and cook until wine nearly evaporates, about 2 minutes. Stir in tomatoes and bring to simmer. Add brisket; cover, reduce heat to medium low, and simmer, turning occasionally, just until tender, about 3 hours.

3 Place brisket on cutting board; thinly slice, keeping shape of brisket intact. Lay slices in sauce in Dutch oven and bring to simmer over medium heat; cover, reduce heat, and simmer until brisket is very tender, about 1 hour.

Per serving (4 slices brisket and 1/4 cup sauce): 207 Cal, 7 g Fat, 2 g Sat Fat, 1 g Trans Fat, 89 mg Chol, 338 mg Sod, 5 g Carb, 2 g Fib, 30 g Prot, 24 mg Calc. ***POINTS*** value: ***4.***

Matzo Farfel with Asparagus and Mushrooms

prep 20 MIN cook/bake 45 MIN serves 12 level BASIC

- 4 teaspoons olive oil
- ♦ 1 pound sliced mixed mushrooms
- 1 teaspoon salt
- ♦ 2 onions, chopped
- 1/2 teaspoon dried thyme
- ♦ 1 pound asparagus, trimmed and cut into 1-inch pieces
- ♦ 1 cup frozen peas
- 6 garlic cloves, finely chopped
- 4 cups whole wheat matzo farfel
- ♦ 1 cup reduced-sodium fat-free chicken broth
- ♦ 4 large eggs, lightly beaten
- ♦ 2 large egg whites, lightly beaten
- 1/2 teaspoon black pepper

1 Preheat oven to 350°F. Spray 3-quart baking dish with nonstick spray.

2 Heat 2 teaspoons oil in large nonstick skillet over medium-high heat. Add mushrooms and 1/4 teaspoon salt; cook, stirring occasionally, until mushrooms brown, about 10 minutes. Transfer to large bowl. Return skillet to medium-high heat and add remaining 2 teaspoons oil. Add onions and thyme; cook, stirring occasionally, until onions begin to brown, 3–4 minutes. Stir in asparagus, peas, and garlic; cook, stirring occasionally, until peas are bright green, 3–4 minutes. Scrape vegetables into bowl with mushrooms. Add farfel and broth, stirring until well combined. Add eggs, egg whites, pepper, and remaining 3/4 teaspoon salt to farfel mixture and stir to combine.

3 Spoon mixture into baking dish and level top. Bake until lightly browned and instant-read thermometer inserted into center registers 160°F, 25–30 minutes. Remove from oven; let cool 10 minutes, then cut into 12 squares.

Per serving (1 square): 142 Cal, 4 g Fat, 1 g Sat Fat, 0 g Trans Fat, 71 mg Chol, 249 mg Sod, 21 g Carb, 4 g Fib, 8 g Prot, 30 mg Calc. ***POINTS*** value: **2.**

Lemon-Dijon Haricots Verts

prep 15 MIN cook 15 MIN serves 12 level BASIC

- ♦ **3 pounds haricots verts (French green beans), trimmed**
- **1 large shallot, finely chopped**
- **3 tablespoons lemon juice**
- **1 tablespoon Dijon mustard**
- **1 teaspoon salt**
- **1/4 teaspoon black pepper**
- **4 teaspoons olive oil**
- **2 teaspoons water**
- **1/4 cup chopped fresh basil**

1 Bring large pot of salted water to boil. Add haricots verts; return to boil and cook 3 minutes. Drain, cool under cold running water, and drain again. Pat dry with paper towels.

2 Combine shallot, lemon juice, mustard, salt, and pepper in large bowl. Slowly whisk in oil. Whisk in water. Add haricots verts to bowl and toss to coat. Stir in chopped basil. Serve at room temperature or chilled.

Per serving (1 cup): 57 Cal, 2 g Fat, 0 g Sat Fat, 0 g Trans Fat, 0 mg Chol, 229 mg Sod, 10 g Carb, 4 g Fib, 2 g Prot, 56 mg Calc. ***POINTS*** value: ***1.***

This recipe works with the Simply Filling technique.

Pear and Apple Haroset

prep 20 MIN cook NONE serves 24 level BASIC

- ♦ 3 pears, peeled, cored, and finely chopped
- ♦ 3 apples, peeled, cored, and finely chopped
- 1 cup pitted dates, finely chopped
- 1/3 cup golden raisins, chopped
- 3/4 cup walnut halves, toasted and finely chopped
- 1/2 cup sweet Malaga wine or grape juice
- 3/4 teaspoon cinnamon

Combine all ingredients in large bowl. Cover with plastic wrap and refrigerate at least 1 hour or up to 24 hours to allow fruits to soften and flavors to blend.

Per serving (1/4 cup): 71 Cal, 2 g Fat, 0 g Sat Fat, 0 g Trans Fat, 0 mg Chol, 2 mg Sod, 12 g Carb, 1 g Fib, 1 g Prot, 9 mg Calc. ***POINTS*** value: ***1.***

IN THE KITCHEN

Sweet, thick haroset is thought to be symbolic of the mortar used by the enslaved Israelites to build the Egyptian Pyramids. It's delicious on its own but is most often eaten in a "sandwich" with horseradish between pieces of matzo. Look for whole wheat matzo in your supermarket; it's a good way to add more whole grains to your diet during the holidays. One piece of whole wheat matzo and 1 teaspoon horseradish in vinegar has a *POINTS* value of *1.*

Coconut Macaroons

prep 20 MIN bake 1 HR serves 24 level BASIC

- ♦ **4 large egg whites, at room temperature**
- **1/2 teaspoon cream of tartar**
- **1/4 teaspoon salt**
- **3/4 cup sugar**
- **1/4 teaspoon coconut extract**
- **1/4 teaspoon almond extract**
- **1 cup sweetened coconut flakes**
- **1/4 cup sliced almonds, chopped**

1 Preheat oven to 250°F. Line 2 large baking sheets with parchment paper.

2 Combine egg whites, cream of tartar, and salt in large bowl. Beat with electric mixer on high speed until soft peaks form. With mixer running, add sugar, 1 tablespoon at a time. Beat until stiff peaks form. Beat in coconut extract and almond extract. Fold in coconut flakes and sliced almonds with rubber spatula.

3 Drop batter by level tablespoonfuls onto baking sheets. Bake until macaroons are dried, about 1 hour, rotating baking sheets top to bottom after 30 minutes. Cool on baking sheets. With a spatula, gently lift macaroons from paper; store in airtight container up to 3 days.

Per serving (3 macaroons): 48 Cal, 2 g Fat, 1 g Sat Fat, 0 g Trans Fat, 0 mg Chol, 41 mg Sod, 8 g Carb, 0 g Fib, 1 g Prot, 3 mg Calc. ***POINTS*** value: ***1.***

Mother's Day Brunch

Bellini Punch

prep 15 MIN cook NONE serves 6 level BASIC

- ♦ **2 ripe peaches, halved, peeled, pitted, and sliced**
- **2 tablespoons sugar**
- **4 teaspoons lemon juice**
- **1 (750-milliliter) bottle prosecco or other sparkling wine, chilled**
- **2 tablespoons peach schnapps**

1 In blender, combine peaches, sugar, and lemon juice; puree until smooth. Pour mixture into small bowl and cover with plastic wrap, pressing plastic against surface of puree to prevent browning. Refrigerate until cold, at least 1 hour or up to 2 days.

2 Combine peach puree, prosecco, and schnapps in pitcher and stir gently. Fill champagne or wine glasses with ice and pour prosecco mixture over ice. Serve at once.

Per serving (2/3 cup): 128 Cal, 0 g Fat, 0 g Sat Fat, 0 g Trans Fat, 0 mg Chol, 8 mg Sod, 9 g Carb, 1 g Fib, 0 g Prot, 13 mg Calc. ***POINTS*** value: ***2.***

IN THE KITCHEN

Very ripe peaches are essential for getting the bright flavor that makes this cocktail great. A sweet, lightly fruity Italian prosecco goes especially well with the peaches, but any light sparkling wine will work in this recipe.

Mother's Day Brunch
MENU FOR SIX

2 DAYS AHEAD
- ☐ Make peach puree for Bellini Punch.
- ☐ Make sauce for Fruit Kebabs with Creamy Raspberry Sauce.

1 DAY AHEAD
- ☐ Bake Deep-Chocolate Chiffon Cake; cool, wrap tightly in plastic wrap, and store at room temperature.
- ☐ Make pie dough for Swiss Chard Tart with Feta and Pine Nuts; wrap in plastic wrap and refrigerate.

EARLY IN THE DAY
- ☐ Make Swiss chard tart; store at room temperature up to 6 hours.
- ☐ Chill prosecco for punch.
- ☐ Make Spring Garden Salad, leaving out avocado and dill; refrigerate.

1 HOUR AHEAD
- ☐ Make fruit kebabs; refrigerate.

LAST MINUTE
- ☐ Add avocado and dill to salad; place lettuce leaves on platter and spoon salad over top.
- ☐ Mix and serve punch.

Swiss Chard Tart with Feta and Pine Nuts

prep 30 MIN bake/cook 1 HR serves 12 level ADVANCED

- **1 cup whole wheat pastry flour**
- **1 cup all-purpose flour**
- **1 tablespoon fennel seeds**
- **1/2 teaspoon salt**
- **1/4 cup olive oil**
- **4–5 tablespoons cold water**
- ♦ **1 1/2 pounds Swiss chard, stems and leaves separated and each coarsely chopped**
- **3 garlic cloves, minced**
- ♦ **1/2 cup reduced-sodium vegetable broth**
- **1 cup part-skim ricotta cheese**
- ♦ **1 large egg**
- ♦ **2 large egg whites**
- **1/4 cup crumbled reduced-fat feta cheese**
- **1/4 cup chopped fresh dill**
- **8 oil-cured black olives, pitted and chopped**
- **1 tablespoon toasted pine nuts**

1 Preheat oven to 400°F.

2 To make crust, put whole wheat flour, all-purpose flour, fennel seeds, and salt in food processor; pulse until blended. Pour oil through feed tube and pulse until mixture resembles coarse crumbs. Pour water, 1 tablespoon at a time, through feed tube and pulse until dough forms. Turn dough onto lightly floured surface; roll out to 13-inch circle and ease it into 11-inch tart pan with removable bottom, pressing dough evenly onto bottom and up sides of pan. Prick all over with fork. Roll rolling pin over rim of pan to cut off overhanging dough.

3 Line tart shell with foil; fill with pie weights or dried beans. Bake until dough looks dried around edges, about 20 minutes; remove foil and weights. Return tart shell to oven and continue to bake just until dough is golden, 10–12 minutes longer. Cool crust in pan on rack 10 minutes.

4 Meanwhile, to make filling, spray large nonstick skillet with nonstick spray and set over medium-high heat. Add Swiss chard stems and cook, stirring occasionally, until tender, about 10 minutes. Add garlic and cook 2 minutes. Add Swiss chard leaves and broth; bring to boil. Reduce heat and simmer, covered, stirring occasionally, until stems and leaves are very tender, 10–12 minutes. Pour mixture through large sieve set over bowl; let drain 10 minutes.

5 Whisk together ricotta, egg, and egg whites in large bowl. Stir in feta, dill, and olives. Stir in chard mixture. Spoon filling into cooled crust and sprinkle with pine nuts. Bake until top is browned and puffed, about 30 minutes. Let cool at least 10 minutes. Remove tart ring and cut tart into 12 slices. Serve warm or at room temperature.

Per serving (1 slice): 170 Cal, 8 g Fat, 2 g Sat Fat, 0 g Trans Fat, 25 mg Chol, 321 mg Sod, 18 g Carb, 2 g Fib, 7 g Prot, 109 mg Calc. ***POINTS*** value: ***4.***

SWISS CHARD TART WITH FETA AND PINE NUTS

Fruit Kebabs with Creamy Raspberry Sauce

prep 30 MIN cook NONE serves 6 level BASIC

- ♦ **2 cups frozen unsweetened raspberries, thawed**
- ♦ **1/4 cup plain fat-free Greek yogurt**
- **3 tablespoons honey**
- ♦ **1/4 cantaloupe, peeled, seeded, and cut into large chunks**
- ♦ **1/4 honeydew melon, peeled, seeded, and cut into large chunks**
- ♦ **1 kiwi, peeled and cut into chunks**
- ♦ **12 strawberries, hulled**
- ♦ **1 banana, cut into 1-inch chunks**
- ♦ **3/4 cup large red seedless grapes**

1 To make sauce, pulse raspberries in food processor until pureed. Strain puree through sieve set over bowl; discard seeds. Stir yogurt and honey into puree. Cover and refrigerate.

2 To make kebabs, thread fruits evenly on 6 (10-inch) wooden skewers. (Fruit can be skewered 1–2 hours ahead, covered, and refrigerated.) Serve with sauce on the side.

Per serving (1 skewer and 2½ tablespoons sauce): 120 Cal, 1 g Fat, 0 g Sat Fat, 0 g Trans Fat, 0 mg Chol, 13 mg Sod, 29 g Carb, 5 g Fib, 2 g Prot, 32 mg Calc. ***POINTS*** value: ***2.***

Spring Garden Salad

prep 25 MIN cook 5 MIN serves 6 level BASIC

- ♦ 1 bunch asparagus, trimmed and cut into 1-inch pieces
- 3 tablespoons unseasoned rice vinegar
- 1 tablespoon olive oil
- 1 teaspoon Dijon mustard
- 1/2 teaspoon salt
- 1/4 teaspoon black pepper
- ♦ 2 celery stalks, diced
- ♦ 1 cucumber, peeled, seeded, and diced
- ♦ 1 pint grape tomatoes, halved
- ♦ 6 radishes, halved and sliced
- ♦ 1 large carrot, shredded
- ♦ 1/3 cup chopped red onion
- ♦ 1 avocado, halved, peeled, pitted, and diced
- 1/4 cup chopped fresh dill
- ♦ Large leaves from 1 head romaine lettuce

1 Bring medium pot two thirds full of water to boil. Add asparagus and cook 1 minute; drain, cool under cold running water, and drain again. Pat dry with paper towels.

2 In large bowl, whisk together vinegar, oil, mustard, salt, and pepper. Add asparagus, celery, cucumber, tomatoes, radishes, carrot, and onion; toss to coat. Cover and refrigerate at least 30 minutes or up to 4 hours.

3 Just before serving, stir avocado and dill into salad. Line a platter with lettuce leaves and spoon salad over top.

Per serving (1 1/4 cups): 115 Cal, 7 g Fat, 1 g Sat Fat, 0 g Trans Fat, 0 mg Chol, 241 mg Sod, 12 g Carb, 5 g Fib, 4 g Prot, 36 mg Calc. ***POINTS*** value: ***2.***

CHANGE IT UP

To give this salad an Asian accent, replace the olive oil with nutty-flavored sunflower oil, use 3/4 teaspoon peeled grated fresh ginger in place of the mustard, and use chopped fresh cilantro instead of dill. The *POINTS* value will remain the same. This recipe works with the Simply Filling technique.

DEEP-CHOCOLATE CHIFFON CAKE

Deep-Chocolate Chiffon Cake

prep 30 MIN bake 1 HR 5 MIN serves 16 level INTERMEDIATE

- **3 ounces bittersweet chocolate, chopped**
- **1/2 cup Dutch process cocoa**
- **1 cup boiling water**
- **2 cups all-purpose flour**
- **2 teaspoons baking powder**
- **3/4 teaspoon salt**
- **1 1/2 cups granulated sugar**
- ♦ **4 large eggs, separated**
- **1/3 cup canola oil**
- ♦ **3 large egg whites**
- **1/2 teaspoon cream of tartar**
- **1 tablespoon confectioners' sugar**

1 Preheat oven to 325°F. Combine chocolate and cocoa in medium bowl; pour in boiling water and let stand 5 minutes. Whisk until chocolate is melted and smooth. Let cool.

2 Whisk together flour, baking powder, salt, and 1 cup granulated sugar in large bowl. Add 4 egg yolks and oil to cooled cocoa mixture and whisk until blended. Stir cocoa mixture into flour mixture.

3 Combine the 7 egg whites and cream of tartar in another large bowl. Beat with electric mixer on medium-high speed until soft peaks form. With mixer on high speed, very gradually add remaining 1/2 cup granulated sugar, beating until stiff peaks form.

4 Stir one fourth of egg whites into chocolate batter. Pour batter over whites remaining in bowl and gently fold together with rubber spatula, folding just until no white streaks remain. Pour batter into ungreased 10-inch tube pan with removable bottom; level top. Bake until cake springs back when pressed lightly, about 1 hour 5 minutes. Let cake cool upside down by fitting tube over neck of wine bottle or by resting pan on 4 upturned glasses.

5 Run a long thin knife around inside and outside edges of pan; remove cake. Dust with confectioners' sugar just before serving. Cut into 16 slices.

Per serving (1 slice): 227 Cal, 9 g Fat, 2 g Sat Fat, 0 g Trans Fat, 53 mg Chol, 184 mg Sod, 36 g Carb, 2 g Fib, 5 g Prot, 22 mg Calc. ***POINTS*** value: ***5.***

♦ FILLING EXTRA

Serve the cake surrounded with fresh spring berries. A 1-cup serving of mixed berries per person will increase the *POINTS* value by *1.*

Father's Day at the Grill

Shrimp Martini with Mango Cocktail Sauce 101

Mixed Grill with Spicy Piri-Piri Sauce 102

Romaine and Tomato Salad with Blue Cheese Dressing 104

Grilled Zucchini with Whole Wheat Couscous 105

Ice-Cream Sundaes with Warm Sautéed Berries 106

Shrimp Martini with Mango Cocktail Sauce

prep 20 MIN grill 5 MIN serves 6 level BASIC

- 2 teaspoons olive oil
- 5 tablespoons lime juice
- ♦ 1 jalapeño pepper, seeded and minced
- 1/4 teaspoon + 1/8 teaspoon salt
- ♦ 24 jumbo peeled and deveined shrimp (about 1 1/4 pounds)
- ♦ 1 1/2 large ripe mangoes, peeled, and pitted
- 1/2 teaspoon grated peeled fresh ginger
- ♦ 3 tablespoons finely chopped red onion
- 1 tablespoon chopped fresh cilantro leaves

1 Spray grill rack with nonstick spray; preheat grill to high or prepare high fire.

2 Combine oil, 2 tablespoons lime juice, half of jalapeño, and 1/4 teaspoon salt in zip-close plastic bag; add shrimp. Squeeze out air and seal bag; turn to coat shrimp. Refrigerate 20 minutes.

3 Meanwhile, make cocktail sauce by combining mangoes, remaining 3 tablespoons lime juice, and ginger in food processor or blender; puree. Transfer to small bowl and stir in onion, cilantro, and remaining half of jalapeño and 1/8 teaspoon salt.

4 Remove shrimp from bag and discard marinade; place shrimp on grill rack and grill until browned and cooked through, 2–3 minutes per side. Serve shrimp hot or at room temperature with mango sauce.

Per serving (4 shrimp and 1/4 cup sauce): 124 Cal, 2 g Fat, 0 g Sat Fat, 0 g Trans Fat, 140 mg Chol, 308 mg Sod, 11 g Carb, 1 g Fib, 15 g Prot, 36 mg Calc. ***POINTS*** value: **2.**

IN THE KITCHEN

For a classic presentation, ladle the sauce into martini glasses or wide, shallow champagne glasses (coupes, not flutes) and hook the shrimp over the edges of the glasses. This recipe works with the Simply Filling technique.

Father's Day at the Grill

MENU FOR SIX

1 TO 2 DAYS AHEAD

- ☐ Make cocktail sauce for Shrimp Martini with Mango Cocktail Sauce; refrigerate.
- ☐ Toast croutons and make dressing for Romaine and Tomato Salad with Blue Cheese Dressing. Store croutons in airtight container; refrigerate dressing.
- ☐ Make sautéed berries for Ice-Cream Sundaes with Warm Sautéed Berries; let cool and refrigerate.

EARLY IN THE DAY

- ☐ Give your grill the once-over to make sure it's clean and all supplies and utensils are handy.
- ☐ Make sauce for Mixed Grill with Spicy Piri-Piri Sauce and refrigerate; marinate steak and pork.
- ☐ Make couscous for Grilled Zucchini with Whole Wheat Couscous; cover and leave at room temperature. Cut and marinate zucchini.

30 MINUTES AHEAD

- ☐ Finish making salad.
- ☐ Marinate shrimp for shrimp martini.

LAST MINUTE

- ☐ Grill shrimp and assemble shrimp martinis.
- ☐ Grill zucchini, make sauce, and transfer to a platter with couscous.
- ☐ Grill steak, pork, and sausage for mixed grill.
- ☐ Reheat sautéed berries before serving sundaes.

Mixed Grill with Spicy Piri-Piri Sauce

prep 15 MIN grill 10 MIN serves 6 level INTERMEDIATE

- ♦ **2 red bell peppers, chopped**
- ♦ **1 jalapeño pepper**
- **2 tablespoons lime juice**
- **2 teaspoons olive oil**
- **2 teaspoons sugar**
- **3/4 teaspoon salt**
- **2 garlic cloves, minced**
- **1 teaspoon ground cumin**
- ♦ **3/4 pound flank steak, trimmed**
- ♦ **3/4 pound pork tenderloin, trimmed and cut into 18 cubes**
- **3/4 pound Italian-style low-fat chicken sausage**

1 Combine bell peppers, jalapeño, lime juice, oil, sugar, and 1/4 teaspoon salt in blender; puree. Measure out and refrigerate 1 cup sauce. Transfer remaining sauce to zip-close plastic bag; add garlic and cumin. Add flank steak and pork tenderloin cubes. Squeeze out air and seal bag; turn to coat meat. Refrigerate, turning bag occasionally, at least 2 hours or up to 8 hours.

2 Spray grill rack with nonstick spray; preheat grill to medium or prepare a medium fire.

3 Remove steak and pork from marinade; discard marinade. Thread pork on metal skewers. Sprinkle pork and flank steak with remaining 1/2 teaspoon salt. Place skewers, steak, and sausages on grill rack; grill steak until well marked and instant-read thermometer inserted into side registers 145°F for medium rare, 5–6 minutes per side; transfer to cutting board and let stand 10 minutes. Grill skewers, turning frequently, until cooked through, about 8 minutes. Grill sausages until they are well marked and skin blisters slightly, about 8 minutes.

4 Transfer pork skewers and sausages to cutting board with steak. Slice steak across grain into 12 thin slices and transfer to platter. Remove pork from skewers and place on platter. Slice each sausage into 6 pieces and transfer to platter. Transfer reserved 1 cup sauce to small bowl and place in center of platter.

Per serving (2 slices steak, 3 pieces pork, 3 pieces sausage, and 2½ tablespoons sauce): 267 Cal, 12 g Fat, 4 g Sat Fat, 0 g Trans Fat, 109 mg Chol, 530 mg Sod, 6 g Carb, 1 g Fib, 32 g Prot, 14 mg Calc. ***POINTS*** value: ***6.***

IN THE KITCHEN

Piri-piri is as ubiquitous on the Portuguese table as ketchup is in this country, and serving grilled meats without it is almost unheard of. A classic version would be much heavier on the olive oil than our version is, and it would be considerably hotter. If you'd like to up the heat of your sauce, replace the jalapeño with a spicier chile pepper, such as a cayenne, red finger, red Fresno, or Thai.

MIXED GRILL WITH SPICY PIRI-PIRI SAUCE

Romaine and Tomato Salad with Blue Cheese Dressing

prep 20 MIN bake 5 MIN serves 6 level BASIC

- **4** **ounces French baguette, cut into 3/4-inch cubes**
- **1/2** **cup crumbled reduced-fat blue cheese**
- **1/3** **cup light sour cream**
- **3** **tablespoons fat-free mayonnaise**
- **2** **tablespoons white-wine vinegar**
- **3/4** **teaspoon Worcestershire sauce**
- **1/8** **teaspoon black pepper**
- ♦ **2** **small heads romaine lettuce, chopped**
- ♦ **3** **plum tomatoes, cut into thin wedges**
- ♦ **1** **large cucumber, peeled and diced**
- ♦ **1/2** **small red onion, chopped**

1 Preheat oven to 425°F. Spray baking sheet with nonstick spray.

2 Spread bread cubes on baking sheet. Bake until lightly browned and crisp, 6–8 minutes. Cool on baking sheet.

3 To make dressing, whisk together blue cheese, sour cream, mayonnaise, vinegar, Worcestershire sauce, and pepper in small bowl. Combine lettuce, tomatoes, cucumber, onion, and cooled bread cubes in large bowl. Drizzle dressing over lettuce mixture and toss to coat.

Per serving (2 cups): 137 Cal, 4 g Fat, 2 g Sat Fat, 0 g Trans Fat, 7 mg Chol, 263 mg Sod, 21 g Carb, 3 g Fib, 4 g Prot, 68 mg Calc. ***POINTS*** value: **2.**

CHANGE IT UP

For a Caesar-style mixed salad, make the dressing with 1/3 cup grated Parmesan instead of the 1/2 cup blue cheese and use lemon juice instead of vinegar, then stir in a minced garlic clove. The *POINTS* value will remain the same.

Grilled Zucchini with Whole Wheat Couscous

prep 20 MIN cook/grill 15 MIN serves 6 level BASIC

- **1/4 cup dried cranberries**
- **1 1/3 cups water**
- **1 teaspoon salt**
- **1/4 teaspoon black pepper**
- ♦ **1 cup whole wheat couscous**
- **2 teaspoons grated orange zest**
- **3 garlic cloves, minced**
- **2 tablespoons balsamic vinegar**
- **5 teaspoons olive oil**
- ♦ **2 pounds zucchini, trimmed and cut on diagonal into 1/2-inch-thick slices**
- **1 1/2 cups lightly packed fresh basil leaves**
- **1/4 cup lightly packed fresh mint leaves**
- **1/3 cup orange juice**
- **1 tablespoon lemon juice**

1 Spray grill rack with nonstick spray; preheat grill to medium or prepare medium fire.

2 Combine cranberries, water, 1/2 teaspoon salt, and 1/8 teaspoon pepper in medium saucepan; bring to boil over medium-high heat. Stir in couscous; remove pan from heat, cover, and let stand 5 minutes. Stir in orange zest, cover again, and set aside.

3 Combine garlic, vinegar, 2 teaspoons oil, 1/4 teaspoon salt, and remaining 1/8 teaspoon pepper in zip-close plastic bag; add zucchini. Squeeze out air and seal bag; Refrigerate, turning bag occasionally, at least 10 minutes or up to 8 hours.

4 Place zucchini on grill rack; grill until browned and tender, about 4 minutes per side.

5 Combine basil, mint, orange juice, lemon juice, and remaining 3 teaspoons oil and 1/4 teaspoon salt in blender; puree. Spread couscous over platter, top with zucchini slices, and drizzle herb sauce evenly over top.

Per serving (1/2 cup couscous, 1/2 cup squash, and 1 1/2 tablespoons sauce): 226 Cal, 5 g Fat, 1 g Sat Fat, 0 g Trans Fat, 0 mg Chol, 395 mg Sod, 42 g Carb, 8 g Fib, 8 g Prot, 66 mg Calc. ***POINTS*** value: ***4.***

♦ FILLING EXTRA

Trim 2 bunches large scallions, sprinkle them with salt and pepper, spray lightly with olive oil nonstick spray, and grill along with the zucchini until softened and lightly browned.

Ice-Cream Sundaes with Warm Sautéed Berries

prep 10 MIN cook 5 MIN serves 6 level BASIC

- 1 tablespoon unsalted butter
- ♦ 4 cups fresh strawberries, hulled and sliced
- ♦ 1 cup fresh blueberries
- ♦ 1 cup fresh raspberries
- 3 tablespoons sugar
- 2 tablespoons orange juice
- 1 teaspoon grated lemon zest
- 3 cups vanilla fat-free ice cream
- 3 tablespoons walnuts, toasted and chopped

1 Melt butter in large nonstick skillet over medium-high heat. Add strawberries, blueberries, raspberries, sugar, and orange juice. Cook, stirring occasionally, until berries are softened and juicy, 3–4 minutes. Remove from heat and stir in zest.

2 Divide ice cream evenly among 6 sundae glasses. Top evenly with berry mixture and walnuts and serve at once.

Per serving (½ cup ice cream, ½ cup berries, and 1½ teaspoons walnuts): 215 Cal, 5 g Fat, 1 g Sat Fat, 0 g Trans Fat, 5 mg Chol, 68 mg Sod, 40 g Carb, 6 g Fib, 5 g Prot, 127 mg Calc. ***POINTS*** value: ***4.***

Christmas Eve Feast of the Seven Fishes

Sparkling Limoncello Aperitif

prep 10 MIN cook NONE serves 12 level BASIC

- **3/4 cup limoncello (lemon liqueur), chilled**
- **24 drops aromatic bitters (such as Angostura)**
- **2 (750-milliliter) bottles sparkling wine, chilled**
- **12 thin slices lemon or lemon twists**

Pour 1 tablespoon limoncello, 2 drops bitters, and 1/2 cup sparkling wine into each of 12 chilled champagne glasses. Garnish each with 1 lemon slice or twist and serve at once.

Per serving (1 glass): 157 Cal, 0 g Fat, 0 g Sat Fat, 0 g Trans Fat, 0 mg Chol, 6 mg Sod, 11 g Carb, 0 g Fib, 0 g Prot, 10 mg Calc. ***POINTS*** value: ***3.***

IN THE KITCHEN

Beloved by Italians, limoncello is a lemony liqueur that gets its bright flavor from lemon rind, not from the juice, so it's surprisingly mild and sweet rather than tart. Before making this delicious aperitif, make sure that the wine and liqueur are very cold.

Christmas Eve Feast of the Seven Fishes

MENU FOR TWELVE

3 DAYS AHEAD

- ☐ Make Berry Tiramisu but do not sprinkle with berries or dust with sugar.

1 DAY AHEAD

- ☐ Make bread crumb mixture for Garlicky Baked Oysters; refrigerate.

EARLY IN THE DAY

- ☐ Make Seafood Salad with Fennel and Grapefruit.
- ☐ Chill limoncello, wine and glasses for Sparkling Limoncello Aperitif.
- ☐ Scrub mussels and clams and peel shrimp for Fra Diavolo with Spaghetti; refrigerate.
- ☐ Assemble but do not bake Rosemary-Roasted Cod; cover pan and refrigerate.

1 HOUR AHEAD

- ☐ Prepare Mixed Baby Greens with Oranges.
- ☐ Make Fra Diavolo.

30 MINUTES AHEAD

- ☐ Bake cod.
- ☐ Assemble oysters.

LAST MINUTE

- ☐ Prepare limoncello aperitif.
- ☐ Bake oysters.

Garlicky Baked Oysters

prep 15 MIN bake 10 MIN serves 12 level INTERMEDIATE

- **1/2 cup plain dried whole wheat bread crumbs**
- **2 shallots, minced**
- **1/4 cup chopped fresh parsley leaves**
- **3 garlic cloves, minced**
- **1 tablespoon olive oil**
- **2 cups kosher salt or coarse sea salt**
- ♦ **2 dozen oysters, shucked, on the half shell**

1 Preheat oven to 425°F.

2 Stir bread crumbs, shallots, parsley, garlic, and oil together in small bowl. Spread salt evenly on large baking pan. Nestle oysters in their shells in salt to keep them level. Spoon about 2 teaspoons bread crumb mixture over each oyster; spray lightly with nonstick spray. Bake until oysters are cooked through and topping is golden, about 10 minutes. Place oysters on platter; discard salt.

Per serving (2 stuffed oysters): 32 Cal, 2 g Fat, 0 g Sat Fat, 0 g Trans Fat, 10 mg Chol, 57 mg Sod, 3 g Carb, 0 g Fib, 2 g Prot, 15 mg Calc. ***POINTS*** value: ***1.***

IN THE KITCHEN

The easiest way to make this dish is to have your fish seller shuck the oysters the day you'll be serving them. You'll get the oyster meat and juice in a tub; ask to have the shells packed separately. When you're ready to cook the dish, choose 24 of the most rounded shells (as opposed to the flatter ones) and place an oyster in each.

Seafood Salad with Fennel and Grapefruit

prep 15 MIN cook 10 MIN serves 12 level BASIC

- ♦ 1 (1-pound) package thawed frozen calamari rings
- ♦ 1 pound bay scallops
- ♦ 1 large fennel bulb, thinly sliced
- ♦ 2 pink grapefruit, peeled and sectioned (work over a bowl to catch any juice)
- ♦ 2 celery stalks, thinly sliced
- ♦ 1 small red onion, thinly sliced
- 1/4 cup fresh flat-leaf parsley leaves
- Zest and juice of 1 lemon
- 1 tablespoon unseasoned rice vinegar
- 1 tablespoon olive oil
- 1/2 teaspoon salt

1 Bring large pot filled two thirds full with water to gentle simmer. Add calamari and scallops and cook just until opaque, about 1 minute. Drain in colander and cool briefly under cold running water. Pat dry with paper towels.

2 Combine calamari, scallops, fennel, grapefruit sections, celery, onion, and parsley in large bowl. Whisk together lemon zest and juice, vinegar, oil, salt, and any grapefruit juice collected in small bowl. Drizzle dressing over salad and toss to coat. Refrigerate, covered, stirring occasionally, until flavors are blended, about 30 minutes or up to 8 hours.

Per serving (3/4 cup): 110 Cal, 2 g Fat, 0 g Sat Fat, 0 g Trans Fat, 107 mg Chol, 221 mg Sod, 8 g Carb, 1 g Fib, 14 g Prot, 42 mg Calc. ***POINTS*** value: **2.**

IN THE KITCHEN

Also known as squid, calamari is available cleaned and cut into rings in the freezer section of most supermarkets. You can also find it fresh in most fish markets; look for it already cleaned, with cartilage and ink removed, or ask the fish seller to clean it for you. Before cooking, separate the tubes from the tentacles, cut the tubes into 1/3-inch-thick slices, and halve or quarter the tentacle sections. This recipe works with the Simply Filling technique.

Rosemary-Roasted Cod

prep 20 MIN roast 25 MIN serves 12 level BASIC

- ♦ 6 plum tomatoes, cut into quarters
- ♦ 2 red onions, cut into 1/4-inch-thick wedges
- ♦ 12 brine-cured Kalamata olives, pitted and chopped
- 4 garlic cloves, thinly sliced
- 1 tablespoon drained capers
- 1 tablespoon + 1 teaspoon chopped fresh rosemary
- 1 tablespoon olive oil
- 1 1/4 teaspoons salt
- ♦ 12 (5-ounce) pieces cod fillet
- 1/2 teaspoon black pepper
- 1/2 cup dry white wine

1 Preheat oven to 400°F. Spray large shallow roasting pan with nonstick spray.

2 Combine tomatoes, onions, olives, garlic, capers, rosemary, oil, and 3/4 teaspoon salt in large bowl.

3 Arrange cod in single layer in roasting pan. Sprinkle with pepper and remaining 1/2 teaspoon salt. Scatter tomato mixture around cod. Drizzle with wine. Roast until tomatoes are softened and fish is opaque in center, 25–30 minutes.

Per serving (1 piece cod with 1/4 cup tomato mixture): 167 Cal, 3 g Fat, 0 g Sat Fat, 0 g Trans Fat, 58 mg Chol, 428 mg Sod, 4 g Carb, 1 g Fib, 29 g Prot, 22 mg Calc. ***POINTS*** value: ***3.***

CHANGE IT UP

This is a terrific dish to make with firm, sweet monkfish, which is particularly well suited to baking. Use 12 (5-ounce) pieces of monkfish tail, and the *POINTS* value will remain the same.

FRA DIAVOLO WITH SPAGHETTI

Fra Diavolo with Spaghetti

prep 15 MIN cook 25 MIN serves 12 level INTERMEDIATE

- ♦ 1 **pound whole wheat spaghetti**
- 1 **tablespoon olive oil**
- ♦ 2 **dozen mussels, scrubbed and debearded**
- ♦ 1 **dozen littleneck clams, scrubbed**
- ♦ 3/4 **pound large shrimp, peeled and deveined**
- ♦ 1 **(28-ounce) can Italian peeled tomatoes**
- 1/2 **cup dry white wine**
- 4 **garlic cloves, finely chopped**
- 3/4 **teaspoon salt**
- 3/4 **teaspoon red pepper flakes**
- 1/4 **cup chopped fresh flat-leaf parsley**

1 Prepare spaghetti according to package directions, omitting salt if desired. Drain.

2 Meanwhile, heat oil in large nonstick skillet over medium-high heat. Add mussels and clams; cover and cook until they begin to open, about 4 minutes for mussels, 3–4 minutes longer for clams. Transfer with tongs to large bowl as they open. Discard any that do not open.

3 Add shrimp to skillet and cook, stirring occasionally, just until opaque in center, about 3 minutes. Transfer to bowl with mussels and clams.

4 Add tomatoes, wine, garlic, salt, and pepper flakes to skillet; bring to boil. Cook, uncovered, stirring occasionally and breaking up tomatoes with side of spoon, until sauce thickens slightly, 8–10 minutes.

5 Stir parsley into sauce. Return seafood to skillet and heat thoroughly through. Transfer spaghetti to large serving bowl. Spoon seafood and sauce over pasta and serve at once.

Per serving (1 1/2 cups): 209 Cal, 3 g Fat, 1 g Sat Fat, 0 g Trans Fat, 56 mg Chol, 417 mg Sod, 31 g Carb, 5 g Fib, 16 g Prot, 52 mg Calc. ***POINTS*** value: ***4.***

Mixed Baby Greens with Oranges

prep 20 MIN cook NONE serves 12 level BASIC

- ♦ **2 (8-ounce) packages mixed baby greens (about 10 cups)**
- ♦ **2 navel oranges, peeled and cut into sections**
- **1/4 cup orange juice**
- **2 tablespoons apple cider vinegar**
- **1 shallot, minced**
- **1 tablespoon honey**
- **1 tablespoon olive oil**
- **2 teaspoons Dijon mustard**
- **1/2 teaspoon salt**

Put baby greens and oranges in large bowl. Whisk orange juice, vinegar, shallot, honey, oil, mustard, and salt together in small bowl. Drizzle dressing over salad and toss gently to coat.

Per serving (1 cup): 37 Cal, 1 g Fat, 0 g Sat Fat, 0 g Trans Fat, 0 mg Chol, 128 mg Sod, 6 g Carb, 1 g Fib, 1 g Prot, 33 mg Calc. ***POINTS*** value: ***1.***

IN THE KITCHEN

We suggest using a precut, prewashed baby green mix in this salad because it saves time, but your own mix of leaf lettuces, radicchio, and endive would work terrifically as well.

Berry Tiramisu

prep 25 MIN cook NONE serves 12 level INTERMEDIATE

- 1/2 cup boiling water
- 1 tablespoon + 1 teaspoon instant-espresso powder
- 1 tablespoon granulated sugar
- 3 tablespoons coffee-flavored liqueur
- ♦ 1 cup plain fat-free Greek yogurt
- 1 tablespoon grated orange zest
- 1 teaspoon vanilla extract
- 1/2 cup + 2 teaspoons confectioners' sugar
- 1 cup thawed frozen fat-free whipped topping
- 2 (3-ounce) packages ladyfingers (48 ladyfingers)
- ♦ 1 cup fresh or frozen unsweetened sliced strawberries
- ♦ 1 cup fresh or frozen unsweetened blueberries

1 Combine boiling water, espresso powder, and granulated sugar in medium bowl; stir until espresso powder and sugar dissolve. Stir in liqueur; let cool slightly.

2 Combine yogurt, orange zest, vanilla, and 1/2 cup confectioners' sugar in large bowl. Gently fold in whipped topping.

3 Line bottom of 3-quart baking dish with half of ladyfingers. Brush with half of espresso mixture to saturate. Top with half of yogurt mixture. Repeat with remaining ladyfingers, espresso mixture, and yogurt mixture. Cover with plastic wrap, being careful not to let wrap touch surface of tiramisu; refrigerate until chilled, at least 4 hours or up to 3 days.

4 Just before serving, sprinkle tiramisu with berries and dust with remaining 2 teaspoons confectioners' sugar. Cut into 12 squares.

Per serving (1 square): 122 Cal, 1 g Fat, 1 g Sat Fat, 0 g Trans Fat, 52 mg Chol, 32 mg Sod, 22 g Carb, 1 g Fib, 3 g Prot, 24 mg Calc. ***POINTS*** value: ***2.***

Fabulous Festivities

CHAPTER 3

Mardi Gras Bash

New Orleans Rum Punch

prep 10 MIN cook NONE serves 4 level BASIC

- **1 cup orange juice**
- **1 cup pineapple juice**
- **1/3 cup golden rum**
- **1/4 cup lime juice**
- **2 tablespoons grenadine**
- ♦ **1 orange, halved, seeded, and thinly sliced (optional)**

In large pitcher, stir orange juice, pineapple juice, rum, lime juice, and grenadine together. Pour into 4 tall ice-filled glasses and garnish each with orange slices.

Per serving (1 glass): 153 Cal, 0 g Fat, 0 g Sat Fat, 0 g Trans Fat, 0 mg Chol, 9 mg Sod, 27 g Carb, 0 g Fib, 1 g Prot, 20 mg Calc. ***POINTS*** value: ***3.***

Mardi Gras Bash

MENU FOR FOUR

2 DAYS AHEAD

- ☐ Prepare Artichoke Dip with Spiced Pita Chips; refrigerate dip and store cooled pita chips in airtight container.
- ☐ Make Honey-Sesame Benne Wafers.

1 DAY AHEAD

- ☐ Make Celeriac Rémoulade.
- ☐ Prepare seasoning mix for Blackened Catfish.
- ☐ Make and chill pitcher of New Orleans Rum Punch.

LAST MINUTE

- ☐ Make Dirty Rice.
- ☐ Make catfish while rice is cooking.

Artichoke Dip with Spiced Pita Chips

prep 15 MIN bake 5 MIN serves 4 level BASIC

- ♦ 1/2 (14-ounce) can artichoke hearts, drained
- ♦ 1/3 cup canned white beans, rinsed and drained
- 2 tablespoons grated pecorino cheese
- 1 1/2 teaspoons olive oil
- 1/2 garlic clove, finely chopped
- 1/2 teaspoon grated lemon zest
- 1 1/2 teaspoons lemon juice
- Pinch cayenne
- 1 tablespoon chopped fresh parsley leaves
- 2 large multi-grain or whole wheat pita breads
- 3/4 teaspoon Cajun seasoning blend

1 Combine artichoke hearts, beans, pecorino, oil, garlic, lemon zest and juice, and cayenne in food processor; pulse until smooth, stopping once or twice to scrape down sides of bowl. Transfer dip to serving bowl and stir in parsley. Cover and refrigerate.

2 Preheat oven to 375°F. Split each pita in half horizontally to make 2 rounds. Place halves, rough sides up, on ungreased baking sheet. Spray lightly with olive oil nonstick spray, sprinkle evenly with Cajun seasoning, and cut each round into 8 wedges. Bake until wedges are browned and crisp, 7–8 minutes. Serve chips and dip at once, or cover and refrigerate dip up to 2 days and store chips in airtight container up to 2 days.

Per serving (3 tablespoons dip and 8 chips): 142 Cal, 3 g Fat, 1 g Sat Fat, 0 g Trans Fat, 1 mg Chol, 448 mg Sod, 25 g Carb, 5 g Fib, 6 g Prot, 24 mg Calc. ***POINTS*** value: ***2.***

♦ FILLING EXTRA

Serve some crudités, like cucumber and bell pepper sticks, or steamed and cooled green beans or broccoli florets, along with the chips.

ARTICHOKE DIP WITH SPICED PITA CHIPS AND NEW ORLEANS RUM PUNCH, PAGE 119

Blackened Catfish

prep 15 MIN cook 10 MIN serves 4 level BASIC

- ♦ **2 tablespoons cornmeal**
- **2 teaspoons paprika**
- **1 teaspoon cracked black pepper**
- **1 teaspoon seafood seasoning (such as Old Bay)**
- **1 teaspoon ground cumin**
- **1 teaspoon packed light brown sugar**
- **½ teaspoon ground coriander**
- **½ teaspoon onion powder**
- **¼ teaspoon dried thyme, crushed**
- ♦ **1 large egg white**
- **2 teaspoons canola oil**
- ♦ **4 (5-ounce) catfish fillets, preferably wild caught**
- **4 lemon wedges (optional)**

1 On large square of wax paper, combine cornmeal, paprika, black pepper, seafood seasoning, cumin, brown sugar, coriander, onion powder, and thyme. With fork, beat egg white in shallow bowl.

2 One at a time, dip catfish fillets in egg white and then in spice mixture, coating both sides. Heat large cast-iron or nonstick skillet over medium-high heat until very hot. Brush skillet with oil. Add catfish to skillet and cook until browned on the outside and opaque in the middle, about 3 minutes per side. Serve each fillet with 1 lemon wedge (if using).

Per serving (1 fillet): 173 Cal, 6 g Fat, 1 g Sat Fat, 0 g Trans Fat, 82 mg Chol, 113 mg Sod, 6 g Carb, 1 g Fib, 23 g Prot, 27 mg Calc. ***POINTS*** value: ***4.***

CHANGE IT UP

This zesty preparation is also excellent with skinless, boneless chicken breast. Use 4 thin-sliced breast fillets (each a little less than ½ inch thick and weighing about 3 ounces) and cook the chicken until completely cooked through, 3–4 minutes per side. The per-serving *POINTS* value for this variation will be *3.*

Dirty Rice

prep 10 MIN cook 25 MIN serves 4 level BASIC

- 1 teaspoon canola oil
- ♦ 1/4 cup chopped onion
- ♦ 1/4 cup chopped celery
- ♦ 1/4 cup chopped green bell pepper
- ♦ 1/4 pound cremini mushrooms, chopped
- 1 garlic clove, finely chopped
- ♦ 3/4 cup quick-cooking brown rice
- ♦ 1 cup reduced-sodium fat-free beef or vegetable broth
- 1/4 cup water
- 1/4 teaspoon salt
- 1 bay leaf
- 1/4 cup loosely packed fresh parsley leaves, chopped

1 Heat oil in medium saucepan over medium heat. Add onion, celery, and bell pepper; cook, stirring occasionally, until vegetables are lightly browned, 6–8 minutes. Add mushrooms and cook until tender, about 6 minutes longer.

2 Stir in garlic. Stir in rice, broth, water, salt, and bay leaf; bring to boil. Reduce heat to medium low, cover, and simmer until liquid is absorbed and rice is tender, 10–12 minutes. Remove from heat; remove and discard bay leaf and stir in parsley.

Per serving (2/3 cup): 100 Cal, 2 g Fat, 0 g Sat Fat, 0 g Trans Fat, 0 mg Chol, 177 mg Sod, 16 g Carb, 2 g Fib, 4 g Prot, 20 mg Calc. ***POINTS*** value: ***2.***

IN THE KITCHEN

Dirty rice is a classic Southern side dish that usually calls for chicken livers and gizzards. We've streamlined the recipe and used mushrooms instead of the chicken giblets and quick-cooking brown rice in place of long-grain white rice; we think our version captures the dish's rich flavor in a uniquely healthful way. This recipe works with the Simply Filling technique.

Celeriac Rémoulade

prep 30 MIN cook 15 MIN serves 4 level INTERMEDIATE

- ♦ **1 1/2 pounds celeriac (celery root), peeled**
- **1/4 cup fat-free mayonnaise**
- **4 teaspoons Dijon mustard**
- **4 teaspoons finely chopped fresh tarragon leaves**
- **1/4 teaspoon black pepper**
- **Pinch salt**

1 Fill 5-quart pot two thirds full of water and bring to boil over high heat. Have ready bowl of ice water.

2 In food processor fitted with shredding disk or with large holes on box grater, shred enough celeriac to equal 5 cups lightly packed. Add shredded celeriac to boiling water and cook 3 minutes. Drain, transfer to ice water to cool, and drain again, pressing out excess water.

3 In large bowl, whisk together mayonnaise, mustard, tarragon, pepper, and salt. Squeeze as much water as possible from celeriac; add to bowl. Toss to coat, cover bowl, and refrigerate at least 1 hour or up to 1 day to allow flavors to blend.

Per serving (3/4 cup): 80 Cal, 1 g Fat, 0 g Sat Fat, 0 g Trans Fat, 2 mg Chol, 428 mg Sod, 16 g Carb, 3 g Fib, 3 g Prot, 75 mg Calc. ***POINTS*** value: ***1.***

IN THE KITCHEN

If you haven't worked with celeriac before, don't be intimidated: With a heavy knife, cut off the top and bottom, stand the root upright, and slice off all the woody, gnarly skin. After cooking the celeriac, instead of pressing out the excess liquid with your hands, try wrapping it in a clean kitchen towel and gently twisting the towel to wring out the liquid. This recipe works with the Simply Filling technique.

Honey-Sesame Benne Wafers

prep 30 MIN cook/bake 35 MIN serves 24 level INTERMEDIATE

- **1/4 cup honey**
- **1/4 cup sugar**
- **2 tablespoons unsalted butter**
- **1/4 cup all-purpose flour**
- **1/4 teaspoon baking powder**
- **1/8 teaspoon baking soda**
- **3 tablespoons toasted sesame seeds**

1 Preheat oven to 350°F. Line large baking sheet with parchment paper.

2 Bring honey, sugar, and butter to rolling boil in medium saucepan over medium heat, stirring often; boil 1 minute. Remove pan from heat and gradually stir in flour. Stir in baking powder and baking soda (the mixture will foam). Stir in sesame seeds. Set saucepan over pan of barely simmering water to keep batter warm (it will become too thick to work with if allowed to cool).

3 Drop batter by level teaspoonfuls onto parchment-lined baking sheet, making batch of 8 cookies and leaving 3 inches between each (batter will spread considerably during baking). Bake until cookies are lacy and lightly browned, 4–5 minutes; cookies can burn quickly, so watch them carefully.

4 Cool cookies on sheet just until they begin to set, about 1 minute. With wide metal spatula, immediately transfer cookies to rack to cool completely. Repeat with remaining batter, making about 5 more batches and reusing same sheet of parchment. Store cookies in airtight container up to 1 week.

Per serving (2 cookies): 38 Cal, 1 g Fat, 1 g Sat Fat, 0 g Trans Fat, 3 mg Chol, 11 mg Sod, 6 g Carb, 0 g Fib, 0 g Prot, 3 mg Calc. ***POINTS*** value: ***1.***

IN THE KITCHEN

Toasting sesame seeds deepens their flavor and adds a nuttiness to dishes that you won't get with raw seeds. To toast them, preheat the oven to 350°F. Place the seeds on a small metal baking pan and bake, stirring occasionally, until lightly browned and fragrant, about 8 minutes. Transfer to a plate to cool.

Oktoberfest Celebration

Warm German Potato Salad

prep 10 MIN   cook 20 MIN   serves 4   level INTERMEDIATE

- ♦ **1¼ pounds red potatoes**
- **2 teaspoons safflower or canola oil**
- ♦ **1 red onion, chopped**
- **2 tablespoons apple cider vinegar**
- **2 tablespoons coarse-grained mustard**
- **2 tablespoons water**
- **¼ teaspoon salt**
- **2 tablespoons chopped fresh parsley leaves**

1 Put potatoes in medium saucepan and add enough water to cover by 1 inch; bring to boil over high heat. Reduce heat to medium low, cover, and simmer just until potatoes are fork-tender, 13–15 minutes. Drain potatoes and set aside until cool enough to handle. Cut warm potatoes into ½-inch chunks.

2 Meanwhile, heat oil in medium skillet over medium heat. Add onion and cook, stirring occasionally, until tender, about 6 minutes. Stir in vinegar, mustard, water, and salt; bring to boil. Remove skillet from heat, add potatoes, and stir gently with rubber spatula until coated. Fold in parsley.

Per serving (½ cup): 171 Cal, 3 g Fat, 0 g Sat Fat, 0 g Trans Fat, 0 mg Chol, 334 mg Sod, 32 g Carb, 3 g Fiber, 4 g Prot, 24 mg Calc. ***POINTS*** value: ***3.***

This recipe works with the Simply Filling technique.

Oktoberfest Celebration

MENU FOR FOUR

UP TO 2 WEEKS AHEAD

- ☐ Make Black Forest Ice-Cream Loaf.

1 DAY AHEAD

- ☐ Make Hearty Vegetable Slaw, leaving out apples.

1 HOUR AHEAD

- ☐ Add apples to slaw.
- ☐ Make Beer-Braised Bratwursts and Sauerkraut.

30 MINUTES AHEAD

- ☐ Make Warm German Potato Salad.

LAST MINUTE

- ☐ Reheat bratwursts and sauerkraut if necessary.

Beer-Braised Bratwursts and Sauerkraut

prep 15 MIN cook 30 MIN serves 4 level BASIC

- 4 (3-ounce) fully cooked smoked low-fat bratwursts, each cut diagonally into thirds
- ♦ 1 onion, thinly sliced
- 1/2 teaspoon caraway seeds
- 1/8 teaspoon coarsely ground black pepper
- ♦ 1 ripe pear, cut into chunks
- ♦ 1 (16-ounce) bag sauerkraut, rinsed and drained well
- 1 cup amber or dark beer
- 1 bay leaf

1 Spray large nonstick skillet with nonstick spray and set over medium heat. Add bratwursts and cook until browned on all sides, about 5 minutes. Transfer to plate. To same skillet, add onion, caraway seeds, and pepper; cook until onion is lightly browned, 6–8 minutes, stirring occasionally. Add pear and cook until softened, 3–4 minutes longer.

2 Stir sauerkraut, beer, and bay leaf into skillet; bring to boil, lower heat, and simmer until most liquid has evaporated, 10–15 minutes, stirring occasionally. Return bratwursts to skillet and cook until heated through, about 5 minutes. Discard bay leaf.

Per serving (3 pieces bratwurst and 3/4 cup sauerkraut mixture): 217 Cal, 12 g Fat, 4 g Sat Fat, 0 g Trans Fat, 48 mg Chol, 839 mg Sod, 16 g Carb, 2 g Fib, 13 g Prot, 24 mg Calc. ***POINTS*** value: ***5.***

CHANGE IT UP

For Cider-Braised Kielbasa and Sauerkraut, substitute 1 pound turkey kielbasa, sliced into 12 pieces, for the smoked bratwursts; use an apple instead of a pear; and substitute 1/2 cup apple cider and 1/2 cup water for the beer. The per-serving *POINTS* value for the dish with these variations will be *4.*

FROM TOP, CLOCKWISE: WARM GERMAN POTATO SALAD, PAGE 127; BEER-BRAISED BRATWURSTS AND SAUERKRAUT; AND HEARTY VEGETABLE SLAW, PAGE 130

Hearty Vegetable Slaw

prep 20 MIN cook NONE serves 4 level INTERMEDIATE

- **1/3 cup apple cider vinegar**
- **2 1/2 teaspoons sugar**
- **1/2 teaspoon salt**
- **1/2 teaspoon celery seeds**
- **1/8 teaspoon red pepper flakes**
- ♦ **2 cups thinly sliced red cabbage, tough core and ribs removed before slicing**
- ♦ **2 celery stalks, thinly sliced**
- ♦ **2 large carrots, shredded**
- ♦ **2 parsnips or parsley roots, peeled and shredded**
- ♦ **2 Granny Smith apples, unpeeled, cored and cut into matchstick strips**

1 Whisk vinegar, sugar, salt, celery seeds, and pepper flakes in medium bowl until sugar dissolves. Add cabbage, celery, carrots, and parsnips; toss to coat. Cover and refrigerate to allow flavors to blend, at least 1 hour or up to overnight.

2 Stir in apples just before serving.

Per serving (1 cup): 112 Cal, 1 g Fat, 0 g Sat Fat, 0 g Trans Fat, 0 mg Chol, 339 mg Sod, 28 g Carb, 6 g Fib, 2 g Prot, 60 mg Calc. ***POINTS*** value: ***2.***

♦ FILLING EXTRA

Stir in a bunch of crisp watercress sprigs with the apples.

Black Forest Ice-Cream Loaf

prep 30 MIN cook NONE serves 12 level ADVANCED

- 1 (1 1/2-quart) container no-sugar-added light vanilla ice cream
- 12 small chocolate wafer cookies
- 1 tablespoon melted unsalted butter
- 1/8 teaspoon almond extract
- ♦ 1 (15-ounce) can dark sweet cherries (packed in water), well drained

1 Spoon 2 cups ice cream into medium bowl; set aside to soften slightly and return remaining ice cream to freezer. Line 8 1/2 x 4 1/2-inch metal loaf pan with plastic wrap, allowing wrap to extend over rim by several inches.

2 Put cookies in food processor and pulse to make crumbs. Transfer crumbs to small bowl and stir in melted butter.

3 Stir almond extract into softened ice cream in bowl; fold in cherries. Spoon ice-cream mixture into lined pan and smooth top; sprinkle with 1/3 cup crumb mixture and press down gently. Freeze until firm, about 2 hours.

4 Remove remaining ice cream from freezer and leave at room temperature just until softened. Remove loaf pan from freezer and gently spread softened ice cream on frozen ice-cream mixture, being careful not to disturb crumbs. Sprinkle with remaining crumb mixture; press crumbs into ice cream. Fold excess plastic wrap over top of loaf to cover and freeze until firm enough to slice, at least 8 hours. This ice-cream loaf can be made up to 2 weeks ahead.

5 To serve, unwrap plastic at top of loaf. Invert loaf on platter and remove and discard plastic wrap. Cut loaf into 12 slices.

Per serving (1 slice): 153 Cal, 6 g Fat, 3 g Sat Fat, 0 g Trans Fat, 14 mg Chol, 93 mg Sod, 22 g Carb, 0 g Fib, 4 g Prot, 133 mg Calc. ***POINTS*** value: ***4.***

IN THE KITCHEN

The neatest way to cut an ice-cream loaf is to have at hand a long slicing knife, a tall glass of hot water, and a kitchen towel. First dip your knife into the hot water, wipe it dry on the towel, and cut your slice. Repeat the process for each slice. You can do this before dinner and place each slice on a plate and place the plates in the freezer.

Kids' Halloween Party

Eyeball Punch

prep 30 MIN cook NONE serves 12 level INTERMEDIATE

- ♦ 3 large firm-ripe pears, peeled
- Few drops red food coloring (optional)
- 36 dried currants
- 1 quart white grape juice, chilled
- 1 quart apple juice, chilled
- 1/4 cup lemon juice, chilled
- 2 tablespoons honey
- 1 (1-liter) bottle seltzer, chilled

1 With small melon baller, scoop out 36 balls from pears, making sure to avoid cores; transfer balls to medium bowl. If using food coloring, add to bowl and toss balls to distribute coloring; this will give "eyeballs" a bloodshot look. Using tip of paring knife, cut small hole in center of flat side of each ball and insert 1 currant.

2 Combine grape juice, apple juice, lemon juice, and honey in punch bowl or other large bowl and mix well. Pour in seltzer and add pear balls; serve cold.

Per serving (1 cup and 3 pear balls): 118 Cal, 0 g Fat, 0 g Sat Fat, 0 g Trans Fat, 0 mg Chol, 6 mg Sod, 30 g Carb, 1 g Fib, 1 g Prot, 17 mg Calc. ***POINTS*** value: ***2.***

Spooky Graveyard Dip with Veggies

Kids' Halloween Party

MENU FOR TWELVE

2 DAYS AHEAD

- ☐ Make dip for Spooky Graveyard Dip with Veggies but do not decorate; refrigerate.
- ☐ Unless dipping and decorating Caramel Apples will be a party activity, prepare apples; refrigerate.

1 DAY AHEAD

- ☐ Make sauce for Devils' Chicken Fingers with Demon Sauce; refrigerate.
- ☐ Cut vegetables for graveyard dip; wrap in paper towels and then in plastic wrap and refrigerate.

EARLY IN THE DAY

- ☐ Assemble Eyeball Punch, leaving out seltzer; chill.
- ☐ Walk through party area to make sure it is ready for children: Put away items that might break and any that might present a hazard, such as loose area rugs, and clear room of nonessential furniture so that kids have plenty of room in which to move around.

1 HOUR AHEAD

- ☐ Decorate graveyard dip and surround with vegetables.
- ☐ Prepare chicken fingers; refrigerate until ready to bake.

LAST MINUTE

- ☐ Bake chicken fingers.
- ☐ Add seltzer to punch.

prep 30 MIN cook NONE serves 12 level BASIC

- **2 (8-ounce) packages fat-free cream cheese**
- **1 (8-ounce) package light cream cheese (Neufchâtel)**
- ♦ **1/2 cup prepared mild fat-free salsa**
- **1/4 pound shredded low-fat sharp Cheddar cheese**
- ♦ **3 scallions, thinly sliced**
- **3 slices pumpernickel bread, crusts removed**
- **12 reduced-fat crackers**
- ♦ **4 carrots, quartered lengthwise and cut into 2 1/2-inch-long sticks**
- ♦ **4 celery stalks, halved lengthwise and cut into 2 1/2-inch-long sticks**
- ♦ **1 large seedless cucumber, cut into 1/4-inch slices**

1 Line 8-inch-square baking dish with plastic wrap.

2 Remove 2 tablespoons fat-free cream cheese and set aside. Combine light cream cheese, salsa, and remaining fat-free cream cheese in large bowl and beat with electric mixer on medium speed until well combined. Stir in Cheddar and scallions. Spread cheese mixture evenly in baking dish. Cover with more plastic wrap and refrigerate 2 hours or up to 2 days.

3 Remove plastic wrap from top of baking dish and set platter upside down over dish; quickly invert, then remove dish and remaining plastic wrap. Put pumpernickel in food processor and pulse to make coarse crumbs. Spread crumbs over top and down sides of cream cheese mixture; brush any excess crumbs off platter. Spread one side of each cracker evenly with thin coating of reserved 2 tablespoons cream cheese. Insert crackers into dip, cream cheese sides facing you, making crooked rows of "tombstones." Arrange carrot sticks, celery sticks, and cucumber slices around dip.

Per serving (1/4 cup dip, 7 pieces of vegetables, and 1 cracker): 164 Cal, 6 g Fat, 4 g Sat Fat, 0 g Trans Fat, 19 mg Chol, 500 mg Sod, 16 g Carb, 2 g Fib, 12 g Prot, 150 mg Calc. ***POINTS*** value: ***3.***

Devils' Chicken Fingers with Demon Sauce

prep 30 MIN bake 15 MIN serves 12 level INTERMEDIATE

- **1/2 cup light sour cream**
- **1/3 cup light mayonnaise**
- **1/3 cup low-fat buttermilk**
- **1 garlic clove, minced**
- **1 tablespoon apple cider vinegar**
- **2 tablespoons + 1 teaspoon ketchup**
- **2 teaspoons paprika**
- **6 cups cornflakes**
- **1/2 cup all-purpose flour**
- **1 teaspoon chili powder**
- **1 1/4 teaspoons salt**
- ♦ **2 large eggs**
- ♦ **3 large egg whites**
- ♦ **3 pounds skinless, boneless chicken breast, cut into 60 (1/4-inch-thick) strips**

1 Preheat oven to 375°F. Spray 2 large baking sheets with nonstick spray.

2 Whisk together sour cream, mayonnaise, buttermilk, garlic, vinegar, 2 tablespoons ketchup, and 1 teaspoon paprika in small bowl. Transfer to serving bowl and dollop remaining 1 teaspoon ketchup in center.

3 Put cornflakes in food processor or blender and pulse to make fine crumbs; transfer to shallow bowl. In medium bowl, combine flour, chili powder, salt, and remaining 1 teaspoon paprika. Whisk together eggs and egg whites in third bowl. Add chicken strips to flour mixture and toss to coat. Working with one strip at a time, shake off excess flour, dip in egg mixture, then dredge in cornflakes. Place coated strips on prepared baking sheets.

4 Spray chicken strips lightly with nonstick spray. Bake 7 minutes; turn strips with tongs, then rotate pans top to bottom and bake until strips are golden and cooked through, 7–8 minutes longer. Serve warm with sauce.

Per serving (5 chicken fingers and 1 1/2 tablespoons sauce): 248 Cal, 7 g Fat, 2 g Sat Fat, 0 g Trans Fat, 104 mg Chol, 579 mg Sod, 18 g Carb, 1 g Fib, 27 g Prot, 48 mg Calc. ***POINTS*** value: ***5.***

CHANGE IT UP

If you're looking for a more adult entrée, try Oven-Fried Chicken with Hades Sauce: Substitute hot pepper sauce for the ketchup and replace the chicken breast with 12 small skinless chicken thighs (about 3 3/4 pounds). Leave the thighs whole, coat, and bake about 30 minutes in all, turning thighs after 15 minutes of cooking time. The *POINTS* value per thigh and 1 1/2 tablespoons sauce will remain the same.

CARAMEL APPLES

Caramel Apples

prep 1 HR cook 5 MIN serves 12 level INTERMEDIATE

- ♦ **12 small Gala apples**
- **12 ice-pop sticks**
- **1½ (14-ounce) bags traditional caramels, such as Kraft's**
- **¼ cup orange juice**
- **2 teaspoons vanilla extract**
- **¼ teaspoon cinnamon**
- **Chocolate sprinkles or edible glitter**
- **Dried fruits, such as currants, raisins, cherries, cranberries and pineapple (optional)**
- **Candies such as mini marshmallows, mini-chocolate chips, candy corn, and rope licorice (optional)**

1 Remove stems from apples; rinse and dry apples completely. Insert 1 ice-pop stick into stem end of each apple. Line baking sheet with parchment paper or wax paper and spray lightly with canola oil nonstick spray.

2 Unwrap caramels if necessary. Combine caramels, orange juice, vanilla, and cinnamon in a medium saucepan over medium heat. Cook, stirring constantly, until caramels melt and mixture is smooth, about 5 minutes. Remove from heat. Working with one apple at a time, tilt saucepan to one side and dip apple three quarters of the way into caramel mixture; twirl to coat. Let excess caramel drip back into pan. Scrape off any excess caramel from bottom of apple with table knife. Turn apple right side up and allow caramel to settle. Dip top of apple into sprinkles or glitter, then transfer to baking sheet, stick side up. Repeat with remaining apples.

3 While caramel is still warm, decorate apples with dried fruits and/or candies (if using), making patterns or spooky faces. Refrigerate apples until caramel is firm, 30 minutes or up to 2 days.

Per serving (1 caramel apple without decorations): 256 Cal, 4 g Fat, 3 g Sat Fat, 0 g Trans Fat, 4 mg Chol, 122 mg Sod, 55 g Carb, 4 g Fib, 3 g Prot, 77 mg Calc. ***POINTS*** value: **5.**

Vegetarian Harvest Dinner

Cassis-Cider Blushes

prep 10 MIN cook NONE serves 12 level BASIC

- **2 (25.4-ounce) bottles sparkling "hard" apple cider, chilled**
- **1 1/2 cups crème de cassis, chilled**
- **2 tablespoons lemon juice**
- ♦ **12 apple slices**
- **12 lemon slices**

Have ready 12 champagne flutes or small wine glasses. Pour 1/2 cup cider, 2 tablespoons cassis, and 1/2 teaspoon lemon juice into each glass and garnish each with 1 apple slice and 1 lemon slice.

Per serving (1 glass): 134 Cal, 0 g Fat, 0 g Sat Fat, 0 g Trans Fat, 0 mg Chol, 10 mg Sod, 15 g Carb, 0 g Fib, 0 g Prot, 1 mg Calc. ***POINTS*** value: ***3.***

CHANGE IT UP

For an alcohol-free version of this cocktail, use sparkling nonalcoholic cider instead of hard cider, and substitute 1 tablespoon black currant syrup, blackberry syrup, or grenadine for the cassis in each drink. The per-serving *POINTS* value for this variation will be *2*.

Vegetarian Harvest Dinner

MENU FOR TWELVE

UP TO 1 MONTH AHEAD

- ☐ Make Ginger-Cardamom Sweet Potato Soup, omitting lime zest and cilantro; let cool and freeze.

2 DAYS AHEAD

- ☐ Make Holiday Vegetable Ragout; refrigerate ragout and mushrooms separately.

1 DAY AHEAD

- ☐ Make Roast Stuffed Artichoke Hearts; refrigerate without roasting.
- ☐ Make fruit filling for Mixed Fruit Strudels; refrigerate.

EARLY IN THE DAY

- ☐ Chill cider and cassis for Cassis-Cider Blushes.
- ☐ Bake strudels; store at room temperature.

1 HOUR AHEAD

- ☐ Make Apple, Celery, and Herb Salad.
- ☐ Roast artichokes.
- ☐ Reheat soup. If you like, place hot soup in slow cooker to keep it warm for easy buffet serving. Add lime zest and cilantro.

LAST MINUTE

- ☐ Reheat ragout and mushrooms separately; add mushrooms to ragout.
- ☐ Make cassis blushes.

Ginger-Cardamom Sweet Potato Soup

prep 15 MIN cook 30 MIN serves 12 level BASIC

- 2 teaspoons olive oil
- ♦ 1 onion, chopped
- ♦ 8 cups reduced-sodium vegetable broth
- ♦ 2 1/2 pounds sweet potatoes, peeled and cut into chunks
- 1/4 cup coarsely chopped peeled fresh ginger
- ♦ 1 jalapeño pepper, seeded and chopped
- 3 tablespoons packed light brown sugar
- 1 1/2 teaspoons ground cardamom
- 1/2 teaspoon ground nutmeg
- 1/2 cup light coconut milk
- Grated zest and juice of 1 lime
- 1/4 cup chopped fresh cilantro leaves

1 Heat oil in large nonstick saucepan over medium-high heat. Add onion and cook, stirring frequently, until softened, about 5 minutes. Add broth, potatoes, ginger, jalapeño, brown sugar, cardamom, and nutmeg; bring to boil. Reduce heat and simmer, partially covered, until potatoes are fork-tender, about 20 minutes.

2 Let soup cool 5 minutes; transfer in batches to food processor or blender and puree. Return soup to saucepan. Stir in coconut milk and lime zest and juice; heat through. Serve sprinkled with cilantro.

Per serving (1 cup): 132 Cal, 2 g Fat, 1 g Sat Fat, 0 g Trans Fat, 0 mg Chol, 304 mg Sod, 27 g Carb, 3 g Fib, 2 g Prot, 35 mg Calc. ***POINTS*** value: **2.**

Roast Stuffed Artichoke Hearts

prep 25 MIN cook/roast 1 HR 5 MIN serves 12 level INTERMEDIATE

- **2 lemons, halved**
- ♦ **6 large artichokes**
- **1 1/4 cups multigrain croutons, crushed**
- **1/4 cup finely grated Parmesan cheese**
- **1/4 cup chopped fresh parsley leaves**
- **1 tablespoon chopped fresh oregano leaves**
- **1 tablespoon olive oil**
- **2 garlic cloves, minced**
- ♦ **1/4 cup reduced-sodium vegetable broth**

1 Fill large nonreactive pot two thirds full of water and bring to boil over high heat.

2 Meanwhile, squeeze lemons into large bowl of water; drop in lemon halves. One artichoke at a time, snap off and discard dark green outer leaves, leaving light green leaves exposed. With paring knife, peel tough skin from stem. Slice off and discard top 1 inch of artichoke leaves. Drop artichoke into bowl with lemon water. Repeat with remaining artichokes.

3 Put artichokes and lemon halves into boiling water; return water to boil. Reduce heat, cover, and simmer until paring knife inserted into bottom of artichokes goes in easily, about 20 minutes. Drain artichokes, cool briefly under cold running water, and drain again. Slice each artichoke in half lengthwise and use small spoon to scoop out and discard fuzzy choke and any violet-tipped leaves surrounding choke.

4 Preheat oven to 400°F. Spray 9 x 13-inch baking dish with nonstick spray. Combine croutons, Parmesan, parsley, oregano, oil, and garlic in medium bowl. Fill center of each artichoke half with 1 heaping tablespoon crouton mixture; spray tops lightly with nonstick spray. Place artichoke halves in baking dish. Pour broth around artichokes. Cover with foil and roast 15 minutes. Remove foil and roast until topping is browned, 15–20 minutes longer.

Per serving (1 stuffed artichoke half): 73 Cal, 2 g Fat, 1 g Sat Fat, 0 g Trans Fat, 1 mg Chol, 143 mg Sod, 12 g Carb, 5 g Fib, 4 g Prot, 67 mg Calc. ***POINTS*** value: ***1.***

IN THE KITCHEN

If you'd like to serve the artichokes whole, rather than halved, simply remove the stems and tough outer leaves, trim off any spines with scissors, and put artichokes in the boiling water. When the bottoms are tender, drain well and place each upright in a small baking pan. Spoon the filling between the leaves of the artichokes; bake as directed above. Serve one artichoke per person for a per-serving *POINTS* value of 2.

Holiday Vegetable Ragout

prep 25 MIN cook 30 MIN serves 12 level BASIC

- 4 teaspoons olive oil
- ♦ 2 large leeks, white parts only, thinly sliced and well rinsed
- ♦ 3 baking potatoes, peeled and cut into 1-inch chunks
- ♦ 2 parsnips, peeled and cut into 1/2-inch thick slices
- ♦ 1 1/2 cups baby carrots
- ♦ 1 zucchini, cut into 1/2-inch slices
- 3 garlic cloves, minced
- ♦ 2 tablespoons tomato paste
- ♦ 4 cups reduced-sodium vegetable broth
- ♦ 2 (15-ounce) cans chickpeas, rinsed and drained
- ♦ 1 (9-ounce) bag baby spinach
- ♦ 1 pound oyster mushrooms or other wild mushrooms, trimmed
- 1/2 teaspoon salt

1 Heat oil in large nonstick Dutch oven over medium-high heat. Add leeks and cook, stirring occasionally, until softened, 5–6 minutes. Add potatoes, parsnips, carrots, zucchini, garlic, tomato paste, and broth; bring to boil. Reduce heat and simmer, covered, until vegetables are fork-tender, 20–25 minutes. Add chickpeas and spinach; cook, uncovered, stirring occasionally, until chickpeas are heated through and spinach is wilted, 2–3 minutes. Remove from heat.

2 Meanwhile, spray large nonstick skillet with nonstick spray and set over medium-high heat. Add mushrooms and salt; cook, stirring occasionally, until mushrooms are tender, 5–6 minutes. Serve mushrooms over ragout.

Per serving (1 cup): 155 Cal, 2 g Fat, 0 g Sat Fat, 0 g Trans Fat, 0 mg Chol, 397 mg Sod, 29 g Carb, 6 g Fib, 6 g Prot, 71 mg Calc. ***POINTS*** value: **2.**

IN THE KITCHEN

Mini pumpkin shells make festive natural tureens for this holiday stew. Cut off the tops of the pumpkins and scoop out the seeds and fibers, then spray the insides with nonstick spray. Place the pumpkin shells and lids on an oiled baking sheet and bake in a 375°F oven just until the shells begin to soften, 20–30 minutes (be careful not to bake the shells too long or the walls may become too soft to hold the stew). Ladle the ragout into the pumpkins and serve at once. This recipe works with the Simply Filling technique.

HOLIDAY VEGETABLE RAGOUT

Apple, Celery, and Herb Salad

prep 15 MIN cook NONE serves 12 level BASIC

- ♦ 1 **bunch celery, trimmed and thinly sliced**
- ♦ 2 **Granny Smith apples, thinly sliced**
- 3 **tablespoons orange juice**
- 1/4 **cup lightly packed flat-leaf parsley leaves**
- 2 **tablespoons chopped fresh chives**
- 1 **tablespoon chopped fresh tarragon leaves**
- **Zest and juice of 1 lemon**
- 4 **teaspoons olive oil**
- 2 **teaspoons Dijon mustard**
- 1/2 **teaspoon salt**

1 Combine celery, apples, orange juice, parsley, chives, and tarragon in large bowl.

2 Whisk together lemon zest and juice, olive oil, mustard, and salt in small bowl. Pour dressing over celery and apple mixture and toss.

Per serving (3/4 cup): 56 Cal, 2 g Fat, 0 g Sat Fat, 0 g Trans Fat, 0 mg Chol, 160 mg Sod, 10 g Carb, 3 g Fib, 1 g Prot, 46 mg Calc. ***POINTS*** value: ***1.***

IN THE KITCHEN

Sliced apples will discolor quickly when exposed to oxygen, so be sure to toss them with the orange juice right away—the acid in the juice will help them maintain their color.

Mixed Fruit Strudels

prep 20 MIN bake 25 MIN serves 12 level ADVANCED

- **3 tablespoons all-purpose flour**
- **1/2 teaspoon salt**
- **1/2 cup + 2 teaspoons granulated sugar**
- **2 1/2 teaspoons cinnamon**
- ♦ **2 red plums, pitted and sliced**
- ♦ **1 Granny Smith apple, peeled, cored, and thinly sliced**
- ♦ **1 Anjou pear, peeled, cored, and thinly sliced**
- **1/2 cup dried cranberries**
- **2 tablespoons lemon juice**
- **2 tablespoons finely chopped pecans**
- **14 (9 x 14-inch) sheets frozen phyllo dough, thawed**
- **2 tablespoons confectioners' sugar**

1 To make fruit filling, combine flour, salt, 1/2 cup granulated sugar, and 2 teaspoons cinnamon in large bowl. Add plums, apple, pear, cranberries, and lemon juice; toss well.

2 Combine pecans and remaining 2 teaspoons granulated sugar and 1/2 teaspoon cinnamon in small bowl.

3 Preheat oven to 400°F. Lay 1 sheet of phyllo dough on work surface with a long side facing you. Cover remaining phyllo with damp towel and plastic wrap to prevent it from drying out. Lightly spray phyllo sheet with nonstick spray. Continue layering with 6 more sheets, lightly spraying each sheet with nonstick spray.

4 Spoon half of fruit filling over phyllo, leaving 2-inch border all around. Fold 2-inch borders on short sides of phyllo over filling, then roll up jelly-roll–style, starting with the long side near you and making sure not to make roll too tight and tear phyllo. Repeat with remaining phyllo and fruit mixture, making 2 strudels.

5 Place strudels, seam side down, on large baking sheet. Lightly spray strudels with nonstick spray. Cut four 1-inch slits in top of each strudel to allow steam to escape. Sprinkle strudels evenly with pecan mixture. Bake until filling is hot and phyllo is golden, 25–30 minutes. Cool on baking sheet at least 45 minutes. Just before serving, dust with confectioners' sugar and slice each strudel on diagonal into 6 slices.

Per serving (1 slice): 142 Cal, 1 g Fat, 0 g Sat Fat, 0 g Trans Fat, 0 mg Chol, 226 mg Sod, 32 g Carb, 2 g Fib, 2 g Prot, 9 mg Calc. ***POINTS*** value: ***3.***

MIXED FRUIT STRUDELS

New Year's Eve Cocktail Party

Mango-Pomegranate Sparklers

prep 20 MIN cook NONE serves 12 level BASIC

- ♦ 2 ripe mangoes, peeled, pitted, and diced
- 2 tablespoons sugar
- 2 tablespoons lime juice
- 2 cups pomegranate juice
- 1 (750-milliliter) bottle sparkling wine, chilled
- 1 lime, cut into 12 thin wedges, for garnish

1 Combine mangoes, sugar, and lime juice in blender and puree. Pour into small pitcher and stir in pomegranate juice. Refrigerate until chilled, at least 1 hour or up to 2 days.

2 To serve, pour about 1/4 cup mango mixture into each of 12 margarita glasses. Top each with 1/4 cup sparkling wine, stir gently, and garnish with 1 lime wedge.

Per serving (1 glass): 102 Cal, 0 g Fat, 0 g Sat Fat, 0 g Trans Fat, 0 mg Chol, 6 mg Sod, 16 g Carb, 1 g Fib, 0 g Prot, 9 mg Calc.
POINTS value: **2.**

IN THE KITCHEN

For an extra-festive look, rub the rims of the glasses with a lime wedge and dip in colored sugar before filling.

New Year's Eve Cocktail Party

MENU FOR TWELVE

2 DAYS AHEAD

- ☐ Make mango-pomegranate mixture for Mango-Pomegranate Sparklers.
- ☐ Make green tea mixture for Green Apple Spritzers.
- ☐ Make Sausage and Bulgur–Stuffed Mushrooms; refrigerate.

1 DAY AHEAD

- ☐ Make Sweet Onion, Bacon, and Cheese Tarts; refrigerate.
- ☐ Make Spicy Roast Broccoli and Cauliflower Bites; refrigerate.
- ☐ Make Mocha Fudge Brownies with Pecans.

EARLY IN THE DAY

- ☐ Make salmon mixture for Potato Crisps with Smoked Salmon; refrigerate.
- ☐ Chill sparkling wine and ginger ale for cocktails.

2 HOURS AHEAD

- ☐ Assemble Pita Pizzas Caprese.

30 MINUTES AHEAD

- ☐ Bake pita pizzas.
- ☐ Lower oven temperature to 250°F; reheat cheese tarts, stuffed mushrooms, and broccoli and cauliflower bites.

LAST MINUTE

- ☐ Assemble salmon canapés.
- ☐ Prepare cocktails.

Green Apple Spritzers

prep 10 MIN cook 5 MIN serves 12 level BASIC

- 4 green tea bags (caffeine-free if desired)
- 12 red cinnamon candies
- 4 cups boiling water
- Ice cubes
- 3 cups apple juice, chilled
- 2 (12-ounce) cans ginger ale, chilled
- ♦ 1 Granny Smith apple, cored and cut into 12 thin slices

1 Put tea bags and cinnamon candies in 4-cup glass measuring cup; pour in boiling water and let steep 3 minutes. Remove and discard tea bags; let tea cool to room temperature, then cover and refrigerate until chilled, at least 4 hours or up to 2 days.

2 To serve, fill 12 wine glasses with ice. Combine tea and apple juice in pitcher and pour generous 1/2 cup of mixture into each glass. Top off each with 1/4 cup ginger ale and garnish with 1 apple slice.

Per serving (3/4 cup): 56 Cal, 0 g Fat, 0 g Sat Fat, 0 g Trans Fat, 0 mg Chol, 6 mg Sod, 14 g Carb, 0 g Fib, 0 g Prot, 7 mg Calc. ***POINTS*** value: ***1.***

CHANGE IT UP

Use a flavored herbal tea like cinnamon apple instead of the green tea.

Sausage and Bulgur–Stuffed Mushrooms

prep 30 MIN cook/bake 35 MIN serves 12 level INTERMEDIATE

- ♦ **1/4 cup bulgur wheat**
- **1 cup boiling water**
- ♦ **24 large button mushrooms**
- **1/4 pound spicy Italian turkey sausage, casings removed**
- ♦ **1/2 red onion, finely chopped**
- **1 large garlic clove, minced**
- ♦ **2 cups packed baby arugula or spinach, coarsely chopped**
- **1/4 cup spreadable light garlic-and-herb cheese**
- **3 tablespoons seasoned dried bread crumbs**
- **1/3 cup finely grated Parmesan cheese**

1 Combine bulgur and boiling water in small bowl; let stand 15 minutes. Drain well.

2 Meanwhile, remove stems from mushrooms; set caps aside and finely chop stems. Spray large nonstick skillet with nonstick spray and set over medium heat. Add mushroom stems, turkey sausage, onion, and garlic. Cook, breaking up sausage with side of spoon, until sausage is cooked and mixture is dry, about 8 minutes. Stir in arugula and cook until wilted, about 2 minutes. Remove skillet from heat; let cool 10 minutes. Stir garlic-and-herb cheese, bread crumbs, bulgur, and 3 tablespoons Parmesan into sausage mixture.

3 Preheat oven to 375°F. Spray rimmed baking sheet with nonstick spray. Spoon filling by rounded tablespoonfuls into mushroom caps, pressing firmly. Arrange mushrooms on prepared baking sheet. Sprinkle evenly with remaining Parmesan. Bake until mushrooms are tender, 18–20 minutes. Serve warm.

Per serving (2 stuffed mushrooms): 66 Cal, 2 g Fat, 1 g Sat Fat, 0 g Trans Fat, 8 mg Chol, 181 mg Sod, 7 g Carb, 1 g Fib, 5 g Prot, 47 mg Calc. ***POINTS*** value: ***1***.

CHANGE IT UP

You can replace the bulgur with 3/4 cup cooked brown rice. The per-serving *POINTS* value will remain the same.

SWEET ONION, BACON, AND CHEESE TARTS AND SPICY ROAST BROCCOLI AND CAULIFLOWER BITES, PAGE 156

Sweet Onion, Bacon, and Cheese Tarts

prep 25 MIN cook/bake 35 MIN serves 24 level INTERMEDIATE

- **1 teaspoon olive oil**
- ♦ **1 sweet onion, quartered and thinly sliced**
- **1/4 teaspoon salt**
- ♦ **3 slices Canadian bacon, finely chopped**
- ♦ **1/4 cup fat-free egg substitute**
- **2 tablespoons fat-free half-and-half**
- **1/2 teaspoon Dijon mustard**
- **1/8 teaspoon black pepper**
- **24 frozen mini–phyllo tart shells**
- **1/3 cup finely shredded reduced-fat Swiss cheese**

1 Heat oil in medium nonstick skillet over medium heat. Add onion and salt; cover and cook until onion is softened, about 5 minutes. Uncover and cook, stirring frequently, until onion is golden brown, about 12 minutes. Transfer to plate. Add bacon to skillet and cook until lightly browned, about 2 minutes.

2 Preheat oven to 350°F. In small bowl, whisk together egg substitute, half-and-half, mustard, and pepper. Arrange tart shells on baking sheet. Spoon onions evenly into shells. Sprinkle bacon evenly over onions. Pour about a teaspoon egg mixture into each tart. Sprinkle tops evenly with cheese and bake until egg mixture is set, about 15 minutes. Serve warm.

Per serving (1 tart): 33 Cal, 2 g Fat, 0 g Sat Fat, 0 g Trans Fat, 3 mg Chol, 94 mg Sod, 3 g Carb, 0 g Fib, 2 g Prot, 20 mg Calc. ***POINTS*** value: ***1.***

Potato Crisps with Smoked Salmon

prep 15 MIN bake 25 MIN serves 12 level BASIC

- ♦ 4 small red potatoes
- 1 1/2 teaspoons olive oil
- 1/8 teaspoon salt
- ♦ 1/3 cup fat-free sour cream
- ♦ 2 ounces smoked salmon, finely chopped
- 1 tablespoon chopped fresh dill
- 1/2 teaspoon finely grated lemon zest
- Pinch black pepper
- 1 tablespoon snipped fresh chives

1 Preheat oven to 425°F. Spray large baking sheet with nonstick spray.

2 Trim off and discard thin slice from opposite ends of each potato. Cut each potato into 6 (1/4-inch) slices. Put slices in medium bowl and toss with oil and salt. Arrange on baking sheet in single layer. Bake until browned on bottom, about 12 minutes. Turn with spatula and continue to bake until browned and crisp, about 12 minutes longer.

3 Meanwhile, mix sour cream, salmon, dill, lemon zest, and pepper in small bowl.

4 Top each potato slice with about 1 teaspoon salmon mixture and sprinkle evenly with chives. Serve warm or at room temperature.

Per serving (2 potato crisps): 56 Cal, 1 g Fat, 0 g Sat Fat, 0 g Trans Fat, 1 mg Chol, 131 mg Sod, 10 g Carb, 1 g Fib, 2 g Prot, 14 mg Calc. ***POINTS*** value: ***1.***

This recipe works with the Simply Filling technique.

Pita Pizzas Caprese

prep 20 MIN cook 10 MIN serves 12 level BASIC

- **2 (6-inch) whole wheat pitas**
- **1 tablespoon olive oil**
- **1 large garlic clove, crushed through press**
- **1/4 teaspoon red pepper flakes**
- ♦ **3/4 cup chickpeas, rinsed and drained**
- ♦ **2 large plum tomatoes, thinly sliced**
- ♦ **1 cup shredded fat-free mozzarella cheese**
- **1/4 cup freshly grated Parmesan cheese**
- **1/4 cup lightly packed fresh basil leaves, thinly sliced**

1 Preheat oven to 425°F. Spray large baking sheet with nonstick spray.

2 Split pitas in half horizontally to make 4 rounds. Place, rough sides up, on baking sheet. Mix oil, garlic, and pepper flakes together in cup. Place chickpeas in small bowl and mash with fork. Spread pitas with chickpeas. Arrange tomato slices over chickpeas and brush tomatoes with oil mixture. Sprinkle each pita evenly with mozzarella and Parmesan. Bake until pitas are crisp and cheese is melted, about 8 minutes.

3 Transfer pizzas to cutting board and sprinkle with basil. Cut each into 6 wedges; serve hot.

Per serving (2 wedges): 78 Cal, 2 g Fat, 1 g Sat Fat, 0 g Trans Fat, 3 mg Chol, 183 mg Sod, 10 g Carb, 2 g Fib, 6 g Prot, 115 mg Calc. ***POINTS*** value: ***1.***

♦ FILLING EXTRA

Drain and chop 1 (14-ounce) can artichoke hearts and pat the artichokes dry with paper towels. Spread chopped hearts over tomatoes just before sprinkling with cheese and bake as instructed above.

Spicy Roast Broccoli and Cauliflower Bites

prep 20 MIN roast 20 MIN serves 12 level BASIC

- ♦ 1 **small bunch broccoli, trimmed and cut into small florets**
- ♦ 1 **small head cauliflower, trimmed and cut into small florets**
- 1 **tablespoon olive oil**
- 1 **tablespoon water**
- 1 **teaspoon curry powder**
- 1 **teaspoon Dijon mustard**
- ½ **teaspoon chili powder**
- ½ **teaspoon ground cumin**
- ¼ **teaspoon cayenne**
- ¼ **teaspoon salt**

1 Preheat oven to 400°F. Spray large rimmed baking sheet with nonstick spray.

2 Put broccoli and cauliflower florets in large bowl. Stir oil, water, curry powder, mustard, chili powder, cumin, cayenne, and salt together in cup. Drizzle spice mixture over florets and toss well. Spread florets on baking sheet; roast 15 minutes. Stir and continue to roast until vegetables are tender and begin to brown, about 5 minutes longer. Transfer to platter.

Per serving (about ½ cup): 27 Cal, 1 g Fat, 0 g Sat Fat, 0 g Trans Fat, 0 mg Chol, 77 mg Sod, 3 g Carb, 2 g Fib, 2 g Prot, 24 mg Calc. ***POINTS*** value: ***0.***

This recipe works with the Simply Filling technique.

MOCHA FUDGE BROWNIES WITH PECANS

Mocha Fudge Brownies with Pecans

prep 20 MIN cook/bake 25 MIN serves 16 level BASIC

- **3 tablespoons unsalted butter**
- **1/2 cup unsweetened cocoa**
- **1 1/2 teaspoons instant espresso powder**
- **1 teaspoon vanilla extract**
- **3/4 cup packed light brown sugar**
- ♦ **2 large eggs**
- **3/4 cup all-purpose flour**
- **1/2 teaspoon baking powder**
- **1/4 teaspoon salt**
- **3/4 cup coarsely chopped pecans**

1 Preheat oven to 350°F. Line 8-inch-square baking pan with foil, allowing foil to extend over rim of pan by 2 inches. Spray foil with nonstick spray.

2 Melt butter in medium saucepan over low heat. Remove saucepan from heat and whisk in cocoa, espresso powder, and vanilla. Let cool 5 minutes, then whisk in brown sugar and eggs.

3 Whisk together flour, baking powder, and salt in small bowl. Add flour mixture to cocoa mixture, stirring just until blended. Scrape batter into baking pan and level top. Sprinkle with pecans. Bake until toothpick inserted into center comes out with moist crumbs clinging to it, 20–25 minutes.

4 Cool brownies completely in pan on rack. When cool, lift brownies from pan using overhanging foil as handles; cut into 16 squares. Store in airtight container up to 1 day.

Per serving (1 square): 134 Cal, 7 g Fat, 2 g Sat Fat, 0 g Trans Fat, 32 mg Chol, 61 mg Sod, 17 g Carb, 2 g Fib, 3 g Prot, 23 mg Calc. ***POINTS*** value: ***3.***

Quinceaños Celebration

Marinated Shrimp Merida

prep 25 MIN cook NONE serves 12 level BASIC

- ♦ 3 pounds cooked, peeled medium shrimp
- ♦ 4 large plum tomatoes, chopped
- ♦ 1 large red onion, finely chopped
- ♦ 1 jicama, peeled and diced
- ♦ 2 jalapeño peppers, seeded and diced
- 1/2 cup chopped fresh cilantro
- 1/4 cup lime juice
- 2 tablespoons olive oil
- 1 teaspoon ground cumin
- 1/2 teaspoon salt
- ♦ 8 large romaine lettuce leaves
- Lime wedges

1 Combine shrimp, tomatoes, onion, jicama, jalapeño peppers, cilantro, lime juice, oil, cumin, and salt in very large bowl. Cover and refrigerate at least 2 hours or up to 6 hours.

2 Line large platter with lettuce leaves. Top with shrimp mixture and surround with lime wedges.

Per serving (1 cup salad and 1 lime wedge): 110 Cal, 3 g Fat, 1 g Sat Fat, 0 g Trans Fat, 142 mg Chol, 267 mg Sod, 4 g Carb, 1 g Fib, 16 g Prot, 45 mg Calc. ***POINTS*** value: ***2.***

IN THE KITCHEN

Packages of frozen, cooked and cleaned shrimp are available in the freezer section of most supermarkets. They're a convenient and economical ingredient for feeding a crowd. This recipe works with the Simply Filling technique.

Quinceaños Celebration

MENU FOR TWELVE

2 DAYS AHEAD

- ☐ Bake cake layers for Chocolate-Chip Layer Cake with Creamy Frosting. Wrap layers in plastic and refrigerate.
- ☐ Make Chicken Picadillo with Green Chiles, leaving out almonds; let cool and refrigerate.

1 DAY AHEAD

- ☐ Make pork and sauce for Pork Mole with Cilantro Rice; let cool and refrigerate.
- ☐ Make dressing for Mexican Vegetable-Tomatillo Salad.

EARLY IN THE DAY

- ☐ Make frosting and frost cake.
- ☐ Make Marinated Shrimp Merida.
- ☐ Make vegetable salad and toss with dressing.

30 MINUTES AHEAD

- ☐ Make rice to serve with pork mole.

LAST MINUTE

- ☐ Reheat picadillo; garnish with almonds.
- ☐ Reheat pork mole.

Pork Mole with Cilantro Rice

prep 30 MIN cook 40 MIN serves 12 level INTERMEDIATE

- ♦ **6 dried pasilla chile peppers, seeded**
- **5 cups boiling water**
- ♦ **2 cups reduced-sodium chicken broth**
- ♦ **12 (1/4-pound) boneless center-cut pork loin chops, trimmed**
- **1/2 teaspoon black pepper**
- **2 teaspoons salt**
- **6 teaspoons olive oil**
- **6 garlic cloves, peeled**
- ♦ **2 onions, chopped**
- ♦ **3 large plum tomatoes, chopped**
- **1 teaspoon dried oregano**
- **1 teaspoon ground cumin**
- **1/2 teaspoon cinnamon**
- **2 ounces semisweet chocolate, chopped**
- **6 cups hot cooked white rice**
- **1/4 cup chopped fresh cilantro**

1 Heat large nonstick skillet over medium-high heat. Add pasilla chiles and toast 30 seconds per side. Transfer to medium bowl and cover with boiling water; let stand 20 minutes. Drain and discard liquid. Transfer chiles to blender. Add 1 cup broth and puree; return mixture to bowl and set aside.

2 Sprinkle pork with black pepper and 1 teaspoon salt. Heat 2 teaspoons oil in large, deep pot over medium-high heat. Add 6 pork chops and cook until browned, about 2 minutes per side. Transfer pork to large plate; repeat with another 2 teaspoons oil and remaining chops. Set pork aside.

3 Add 1 teaspoon oil, garlic, and onions to pot; cook until onions are golden, 4–5 minutes. Stir in tomato and cook until softened, about 3 minutes. Add oregano, cumin, and cinnamon; cook until fragrant, about 30 seconds. Spoon tomato mixture into blender; add remaining 1 cup broth and puree.

4 Heat remaining 1 teaspoon oil in same pot over medium heat. Add pasilla mixture, tomato mixture, and remaining 1 teaspoon salt; cook, stirring often, until thickened, about 8 minutes. Stir in chocolate; stir until melted, 1–2 minutes. Add pork chops and turn to coat with sauce. Simmer until pork is cooked through, 6–8 minutes. Sprinkle rice with cilantro and serve with pork.

Per serving (1 pork chop, 1/4 cup sauce, and 1/2 cup rice): 358 Cal, 13 g Fat, 4 g Sat Fat, 0 g Trans Fat, 72 mg Chol, 833 mg Sod, 30 g Carb, 2 g Fib, 29 g Prot, 35 mg Calc. ***POINTS*** value: ***8.***

PORK MOLE WITH CILANTRO RICE AND MEXICAN VEGETABLE-TOMATILLO SALAD, PAGE 165

Chicken Picadillo with Green Chiles

prep 20 MIN cook 20 MIN serves 12 level BASIC

- **4 teaspoons olive oil**
- ♦ **2 pounds ground skinless chicken breast**
- ♦ **2 onions, chopped**
- **4 garlic cloves, minced**
- ♦ **2 bell peppers, any colors, chopped**
- **2 tablespoons chili powder**
- **1/2 teaspoon cinnamon**
- **1/4 teaspoon salt**
- ♦ **1 (28-ounce) can diced tomatoes**
- ♦ **1 (4-ounce) can chopped green chiles, drained**
- **1/2 cup golden raisins**
- **2 teaspoons dried oregano**
- **1/2 cup toasted sliced almonds**

1 Heat oil in large nonstick skillet over medium-high heat. Add chicken, onions, and garlic; cook, breaking up chicken with wooden spoon, until browned, about 8 minutes. Add bell peppers, chili powder, cinnamon, and salt; cook, stirring constantly, until fragrant, about 3 minutes.

2 Add tomatoes, chiles, raisins, and oregano to skillet; bring to boil. Reduce heat and simmer, covered, until flavors blend, about 5 minutes. Sprinkle with almonds.

Per serving (2/3 cup): 187 Cal, 6 g Fat, 1 g Sat Fat, 0 g Trans Fat, 45 mg Chol, 317 mg Sod, 15 g Carb, 2 g Fib, 19 g Prot, 56 mg Calc. ***POINTS*** value: ***4.***

IN THE KITCHEN

Serve the picadillo with tortillas on the side; a medium-size corn tortilla for each serving will increase the *POINTS* value by *1.*

Mexican Vegetable-Tomatillo Salad

prep 30 MIN cook NONE serves 12 level BASIC

- ♦ 2/3 **cup plain fat-free yogurt**
- 1/4 **cup lime juice**
- 2 **garlic cloves, minced**
- 2 **teaspoons ground cumin**
- 1 **teaspoon salt**
- ♦ 2 **(12-ounce) cans tomatillos, rinsed, drained, and chopped**
- ♦ 1/2 **pound cremini mushrooms, chopped**
- ♦ 2 **large yellow bell peppers, chopped**
- ♦ 2 **large zucchini, chopped**
- ♦ 1 **large red onion, chopped**

1 To make dressing, whisk together yogurt, lime juice, garlic, cumin, and salt in small bowl. Cover and refrigerate.

2 Combine tomatillos, mushrooms, bell peppers, zucchini, and onion in large salad bowl. Drizzle with dressing and toss to coat.

Per serving (1 cup): 54 Cal, 1 g Fat, 0 g Sat Fat, 0 g Trans Fat, 0 mg Chol, 266 mg Sod, 10 g Carb, 3 g Fib, 3 g Prot, 51 mg Calc. ***POINTS*** value: ***1.***

This recipe works with the Simply Filling technique.

Chocolate-Chip Layer Cake with Creamy Frosting

prep 30 MIN bake 35 MIN serves 20 level INTERMEDIATE

Cake

- **2 cups cake flour**
- **2 teaspoons baking powder**
- **1/2 teaspoon baking soda**
- **1/2 teaspoon salt**
- ♦ **2 large eggs, at room temperature**
- ♦ **2 large egg whites, at room temperature**
- **1/2 cup granulated sugar**
- **1/2 cup low-fat buttermilk**
- **1/4 cup canola oil**
- **1/2 cup semisweet mini–chocolate chips**

Frosting

- ♦ **1 (15-ounce) container fat-free ricotta cheese**
- **1 (3-ounce) package fat-free cream cheese, at room temperature**
- **3/4 cup confectioners' sugar**
- **1 1/2 teaspoons vanilla extract**
- **Food coloring of choice (optional)**

1 To make cake, preheat oven to 350°F. Spray two 8-inch round cake pans with nonstick spray; line with wax-paper rounds and spray rounds with nonstick spray.

2 Whisk together flour, baking powder, baking soda, and salt in medium bowl. With electric mixer on high speed, beat eggs and egg whites in large bowl until light and thick, about 2 minutes. Gradually beat in granulated sugar, beating until mixture is light and very fluffy, about 3 minutes. Beat in buttermilk and oil on low speed, beating just until blended. Beat in flour mixture, beating just until incorporated. Fold in chocolate chips.

3 Spoon batter into pans and level tops. Bake until toothpick inserted into centers comes out clean, 30–40 minutes. Let cool in pans on racks 10 minutes. Invert layers onto racks; peel off and discard wax paper and cool layers completely.

4 To make frosting, with electric mixer on high speed, beat ricotta, cream cheese, confectioners' sugar, and vanilla in medium bowl until smooth, about 1 minute. Beat in food coloring (if using) a few drops at a time until desired color is achieved.

5 Place 1 cake layer, rounded side down, on serving plate. With narrow metal spatula, spread 1/2 cup frosting over layer. Top with remaining layer, rounded side up. Spread remaining frosting over top and sides of cake. Cut into 20 slices.

Per serving (1 slice): 170 Cal, 5 g Fat, 1 g Sat Fat, 0 g Trans Fat, 24 mg Chol, 199 mg Sod, 25 g Carb, 1 g Fib, 6 g Prot, 88 mg Calc. ***POINTS*** value: ***4.***

CHANGE IT UP

If you prefer to bake this as a sheet cake, use an 11 x 7-inch pan, lining the bottom with strips of wax paper. The baking time should remain about the same.

Romantic Birthday Celebration

Melon and Prosciutto Brochettes 168

Honey-Ginger Roast Carrots 169

Fennel-Spiced Lamb Chops with Couscous 171

Mocha-Hazelnut Pots de Crème 172

Melon and Prosciutto Brochettes

prep 10 MIN cook NONE serves 2 level BASIC

- ♦ **1 cup honeydew melon cubes**
- ♦ **1 cup cantaloupe cubes**
- **3 thin slices lean prosciutto, halved**
- **2 teaspoons grated lime zest**
- **1 tablespoon lime juice**
- **1/4 teaspoon cracked black pepper**

Thread honeydew, cantaloupe, and prosciutto alternately on 4 (6-inch) bamboo skewers. Sprinkle with lime zest and juice and pepper.

Per serving (2 brochettes): 111 Cal, 3 g Fat, 1 g Sat Fat, 0 g Trans Fat, 19 mg Chol, 426 mg Sod, 17 g Carb, 2 g Fib, 7 g Prot, 20 mg Calc. ***POINTS*** value: ***2.***

IN THE KITCHEN

To save on prep time, look for precut melon in the produce section or salad bar of your supermarket.

Romantic Birthday Celebration

MENU FOR TWO

UP TO 3 DAYS AHEAD

- ☐ Make Mocha-Hazelnut Pots de Crème.

EARLY IN THE DAY

- ☐ Make Honey-Ginger Roast Carrots; refrigerate.

1 HOUR AHEAD

- ☐ Assemble Melon and Prosciutto Brochettes; place 2 brochettes on each plate, cover with plastic wrap, and refrigerate.

LAST MINUTE

- ☐ Serve brochettes.
- ☐ Make Fennel-Spiced Lamb Chops with Couscous.
- ☐ Reheat carrots in microwave and serve alongside lamb.

Honey-Ginger Roast Carrots

prep 5 MIN roast 25 MIN serves 2 level BASIC

- ♦ 2 cups baby-cut carrots
- 1 tablespoon honey
- 2 teaspoons grated peeled fresh ginger
- 1 teaspoon olive oil
- 1/4 teaspoon ground nutmeg
- Pinch salt

1 Preheat oven to 425°F. Spray small baking pan with nonstick spray.

2 Combine carrots, honey, ginger, oil, nutmeg, and salt in medium bowl; toss to coat carrots. Spread carrots evenly in pan. Roast, stirring occasionally, until carrots are caramelized and tender, 25–30 minutes.

Per serving (1 cup): 108 Cal, 2 g Fat, 0 g Sat Fat, 0 g Trans Fat, 0 mg Chol, 131 mg Sod, 21 g Carb, 3 g Fib, 1 g Prot, 28 mg Calc. ***POINTS*** value: ***2.***

CHANGE IT UP

This method works well with any number of root vegetables, particularly beets. Simply peel them, cut them into 3/4-inch chunks, measure out 2 cups, and adjust the cooking time if necessary. The *POINTS* value will remain the same.

FENNEL-SPICED LAMB CHOPS WITH COUSCOUS

Fennel-Spiced Lamb Chops with Couscous

prep 10 MIN cook/grill 15 MIN serves 2 level BASIC

- ♦ 1/2 **cup reduced-sodium chicken broth**
- 2 **teaspoons olive oil**
- ♦ 1/2 **cup whole wheat couscous**
- ♦ 2 **scallions, thinly sliced**
- ♦ 5 **cherry tomatoes, halved**
- 1 **tablespoon chopped fresh mint**
- 1 **teaspoon finely grated lemon zest**
- 1 **teaspoon fennel seeds, crushed**
- 1/2 **teaspoon dried oregano**
- 1 **garlic clove, minced**
- 1/8 **teaspoon salt**
- ♦ 2 **(1/4-pound) lamb loin or rib chops, trimmed**

1 Bring broth and 1 teaspoon oil to boil in small saucepan. Stir in couscous and scallions; remove from heat, cover, and let stand 5 minutes. Fluff with fork and sprinkle with cherry tomatoes, mint, and lemon zest.

2 Meanwhile, combine fennel, oregano, garlic, salt, and remaining 1 teaspoon oil in small bowl. Rub both sides of lamb chops with mixture.

3 Spray nonstick ridged grill pan with nonstick spray and set over medium-high heat. Place lamb on pan and cook, turning occasionally, until instant-read thermometer inserted into side of chop registers 145°F for medium rare, 6–8 minutes. Transfer chops to 2 plates; divide couscous evenly between plates.

Per serving (1 lamb loin chop and 1/2 cup couscous): 369 Cal, 10 g Fat, 2 g Sat Fat, 1 g Trans Fat, 45 mg Chol, 345 mg Sod, 48 g Carb, 8 g Fib, 24 g Prot, 66 mg Calc. ***POINTS*** value: ***7.***

This recipe works with the Simply Filling technique.

Mocha-Hazelnut Pots de Crème

prep 10 MIN cook 5 MIN serves 4 level ADVANCED

- **1/4 cup sugar**
- **2 tablespoons cornstarch**
- **2 teaspoons instant-espresso powder**
- **2 cups fat-free half-and-half**
- **2 ounces semisweet chocolate, finely chopped**
- **1 ounce bittersweet chocolate, finely chopped**
- ♦ **1 egg yolk**
- **1 tablespoon hazelnut liqueur, such as Frangelico**
- **1 teaspoon vanilla extract**
- **Pinch salt**

1 Whisk together sugar, cornstarch, and espresso powder in medium saucepan. Slowly whisk in half-and-half, whisking until smooth. Set pan over medium heat; cook, whisking constantly, until mixture thickens and bubbles, 6–8 minutes. Immediately remove saucepan from heat. Stir in semisweet and bittersweet chocolate, stirring until chocolate is melted and smooth.

2 Whisk together egg yolk, liqueur, vanilla, and salt in medium bowl. Slowly whisk half of hot half-and-half mixture into yolk mixture. Add yolk mixture to saucepan and cook over low heat, stirring constantly with wooden spoon, just until mixture thickens, 1–2 minutes.

3 Immediately divide pudding evenly among 4 (5-ounce) ramekins; let cool to room temperature. Refrigerate, covered, until thoroughly chilled and set, at least 3 hours or up to 3 days.

Per serving (1 ramekin): 277 Cal, 9 g Fat, 4 g Sat Fat, 0 g Trans Fat, 56 mg Chol, 139 mg Sod, 43 g Carb, 1 g Fib, 6 g Prot, 171 mg Calc. ***POINTS*** value: ***6.***

IN THE KITCHEN

Pots de crème are traditionally baked and require lots of egg yolks in order to set properly. Our stovetop version uses very little fat, cooks in about half the time, and tastes rich and delicious. One caveat: Be sure to stir constantly (and energetically!) over low heat as you cook the egg yolk mixture; if it becomes too hot, it may curdle. The custards will keep refrigerated for a few days, so save the other two for another evening.

Classic Celebrations

CHAPTER 4

Spring Easter Dinner

Cherry Blossoms

prep 10 MIN cook NONE serves 12 level BASIC

- **1 (750-milliter) bottle white wine, chilled**
- **2 cups black cherry juice, chilled**
- **2 cups orange juice, chilled**
- **1/3 cup orange liqueur**
- **1 (1-liter) bottle club soda, chilled**
- **Ice cubes**
- ♦ **12 fresh cherries with stems (optional)**

In large pitcher, stir wine, cherry juice, orange juice, and orange liqueur together. Gently stir in club soda. Pour into 12 ice-filled glasses and garnish each with 1 cherry (if using).

Per serving (3/4 cup): 113 Cal, 0 g Fat, 0 g Sat Fat, 0 g Trans Fat, 0 mg Chol, 9 mg Sod, 15 g Carb, 0 g Fib, 0 g Prot, 11 mg Calc. ***POINTS*** value: ***2.***

CHANGE IT UP

For a Cranberry-Lime Blossom, substitute cranberry juice for the cherry juice and garnish each drink with a lime wedge or twist. The *POINTS* value will remain the same.

Spring Easter Dinner

MENU FOR TWELVE

UP TO 1 MONTH AHEAD

- ☐ Bake Honey-Wheat Crescent Rolls with Poppy and Sesame Seeds; freeze.

2 DAYS AHEAD

- ☐ Make Spring Vegetable Platter with Red Pepper–Basil Aïoli; wrap tightly and refrigerate.

1 DAY AHEAD

- ☐ Make base for Cherry Blossoms without adding club soda; refrigerate.
- ☐ Make cake and cream cheese filling for Lemon-Strawberry Cream Roulade; refrigerate cake and filling separately.
- ☐ Make dressing and hard-cooked eggs for Steamed Asparagus Mimosa with Dill.

EARLY IN THE DAY

- ☐ Assemble roulade up to 4 hours before serving.

1 HOUR AHEAD

- ☐ Make Seafood Salad Canapés in Endive.
- ☐ Make Rack of Lamb with Lemon-Herb Crust.

LAST MINUTE

- ☐ Add club soda to cocktails and serve over ice.
- ☐ Cook and dress asparagus.
- ☐ Reheat frozen crescent rolls.

Seafood Salad Canapés in Endive

prep 15 MIN cook NONE serves 12 level BASIC

- ♦ 1/4 **pound cooked peeled shrimp, chopped**
- ♦ 2 **ounces (1/3 cup) cooked crabmeat, picked over**
- ♦ 1 **tomato, diced**
- ♦ 1/2 **avocado, halved, peeled, pitted, and diced**
- ♦ 2 **tablespoons minced red onion**
- 2 **tablespoons chopped fresh cilantro leaves**
- 1/2 **teaspoon grated lime zest**
- 1 **tablespoon lime juice**
- 1/4 **teaspoon salt**
- ♦ 24 **large endive leaves (from about 4 heads endive)**

Toss shrimp, crabmeat, tomato, avocado, onion, cilantro, lime zest and juice, and salt together in medium bowl. Lay endive leaves rounded-side down on platter. Spoon 1 heaping tablespoon of seafood mixture into each leaf. Serve at once, or cover and refrigerate up to 1 hour before serving.

Per serving (2 stuffed endive leaves): 37 Cal, 1 g Fat, 0 g Sat Fat, 0 g Trans Fat, 24 mg Chol, 97 mg Sod, 3 g Carb, 2 g Fib, 4 g Prot, 29 mg Calc. ***POINTS*** value: ***0.***

FILLING EXTRA

Add 1 cup rinsed and drained canned black beans and an additional tablespoon of lime juice to the seafood salad; mound 2 tablespoons of the mixture into each endive leaf. The per-serving *POINTS* value will be *1*. This recipe works with the Simply Filling technique.

Spring Vegetable Platter with Red Pepper–Basil Aïoli

prep 30 MIN cook 30 MIN serves 12 level INTERMEDIATE

- 4 garlic cloves, unpeeled
- ♦ 1 (15-ounce) can cannellini (white kidney) beans, rinsed and drained
- ♦ 1 (12-ounce) jar fire-roasted red bell peppers (not packed in oil), rinsed and drained
- 1/3 cup fat-free mayonnaise
- 1 tablespoon lemon juice
- 1/2 teaspoon salt
- Pinch cayenne
- 1/2 cup lightly packed fresh basil leaves
- ♦ 1 1/2 pounds baby potatoes, such as fingerlings, halved
- ♦ 24 peeled baby carrots
- ♦ 2 cups sugar snap peas, stringed
- ♦ 2 bunches baby radishes, trimmed

1 To make aïoli, put garlic in small saucepan and cover with water; bring to boil. Reduce heat and simmer 5 minutes. Drain, cool garlic under cold running water, and remove and discard papery peel. Put garlic in food processor and pulse until minced. Add beans and bell peppers; pulse until smooth. Add mayonnaise, lemon juice, salt, and cayenne; pulse until blended. Add basil and pulse until chopped. Transfer to serving bowl, cover, and refrigerate.

2 Bring large pot of water to boil. Add potatoes and cook until tender, about 15 minutes. Remove with slotted spoon and place on baking sheet lined with paper towels. Add carrots to boiling water and cook 2 minutes. Remove with slotted spoon and place on baking sheet. Add sugar snap peas to boiling water and cook until bright green, about 30 seconds. Drain, cool under cold running water, and place on baking sheet.

3 Arrange potatoes, carrots, peas, and radishes on platter along with bowl of aïoli, for dripping.

Per serving (1 cup vegetables and 3 tablespoons aïoli): 97 Cal, 1 g Fat, 0 g Sat Fat, 0 g Trans Fat, 1 mg Chol, 232 mg Sod, 20 g Carb, 3 g Fib, 3 g Prot, 36 mg Calc. ***POINTS*** value: ***1.***

IN THE KITCHEN

For a more pronounced garlic flavor, simmer only 3 garlic cloves and add 1 raw peeled clove to the food processor along with the cooked garlic. This recipe works with the Simply Filling technique.

Rack of Lamb with Lemon-Herb Crust

prep 25 MIN cook 20 MIN serves 12 level INTERMEDIATE

- **3 garlic cloves**
- **2 slices whole wheat bread**
- **1/4 cup lightly packed fresh mint leaves**
- **1/4 cup lightly packed fresh parsley leaves**
- **1 tablespoon fresh thyme leaves**
- **Grated zest of 2 lemons**
- **1 tablespoon olive oil**
- ♦ **3 (8-rib) racks of lamb, trimmed and frenched**
- **3/4 teaspoon salt**
- **3/4 teaspoon black pepper**

1 Put garlic in food processor and pulse until chopped. Add bread, mint, parsley, thyme, and zest; pulse until finely chopped. Pour oil through feed tube and pulse until combined; set aside.

2 Spray grill rack with nonstick spray; preheat grill to medium high or prepare medium high fire.

3 Sprinkle lamb all over with salt and pepper. Place on grill rack and grill, turning once, until nicely browned, about 5 minutes per side. Transfer lamb to platter. Press herb mixture evenly on meaty (rounded) side of lamb racks; lightly spray herb mixture with nonstick spray. Return lamb, herb side up, to grill and cook until instant-read thermometer inserted into center of each rack (not touching bone) registers 145°F for medium rare, about 10 minutes. (Do not turn lamb.)

4 Transfer lamb to cutting board and cover loosely with foil. Let stand 10 minutes, then slice between every other bone, making 12 double chops.

Per serving (1 double chop): 224 Cal, 10 g Fat, 3 g Sat Fat, 0 g Trans Fat, 87 mg Chol, 249 mg Sod, 3 g Carb, 1 g Fib, 28 g Prot, 31 mg Calc. ***POINTS*** value: ***5.***

FROM TOP TO LEFT, CLOCKWISE: STEAMED ASPARAGUS MIMOSA WITH DILL, PAGE 182; HONEY-WHEAT CRESCENT ROLLS WITH POPPY AND SESAME SEEDS, PAGE 183; AND RACK OF LAMB WITH LEMON-HERB CRUST

Steamed Asparagus Mimosa with Dill

prep 20 MIN cook 5 MIN serves 12 level BASIC

- **3 tablespoons unseasoned rice vinegar**
- **1 shallot, minced**
- **1 tablespoon Dijon mustard**
- **1 tablespoon olive oil**
- **1/2 teaspoon salt**
- **1/4 teaspoon black pepper**
- ♦ **2 hard-cooked eggs, peeled**
- ♦ **3 (1-pound) bunches asparagus, trimmed**
- **2 tablespoons chopped fresh dill**
- **Dill sprigs (optional)**

1 To make dressing, whisk together vinegar, shallot, mustard, oil, salt, and pepper in small bowl.

2 Halve eggs; discard 1 yolk or reserve for another use. Finely chop whites. Press yolk through coarse sieve.

3 Put asparagus in steamer basket set in large pot over 1 inch boiling water. Cover tightly and steam until spears are crisp-tender, about 4 minutes. Transfer to platter. Stir dill into dressing and spoon over asparagus; sprinkle with egg whites and egg yolk. Garnish with dill sprigs (if using).

Per serving (5 asparagus spears and 1 tablespoon egg and dressing): 39 Cal, 2 g Fat, 1 g Sat Fat, 0 g Trans Fat, 35 mg Chol, 97 mg Sod, 3 g Carb, 1 g Fib, 3 g Prot, 18 mg Calc. ***POINTS*** value: ***1.***

This recipe works with the Simply Filling technique.

Honey-Wheat Crescent Rolls with Poppy and Sesame Seeds

prep 30 MIN bake 15 MIN serves 12 level ADVANCED

- **1 cup warm (about 115°F) water**
- **2 tablespoons honey**
- **1½ cups all-purpose flour**
- **1 cup whole wheat flour**
- **1 package quick-rise yeast**
- **1¼ teaspoons salt**
- ♦ **1 large egg, beaten**
- **1 teaspoon sesame seeds**
- **½ teaspoon poppy seeds**

1 Combine water and honey in large measuring cup; stir to dissolve honey.

2 Combine all-purpose flour, whole wheat flour, yeast, and salt in food processor. With machine running, pour water-honey mixture through feed tube; process until dough forms and pulls away from sides of bowl, about 1 minute. Turn dough onto lightly floured surface and knead a few times until smooth. Cover with clean kitchen towel and let rest 15 minutes.

3 Spray large baking sheet with nonstick spray. Dust work surface lightly with flour. Divide dough in half. Roll one half into 10-inch circle. Cut circle into 6 wedges. Starting at wide end, roll each wedge and bend slightly to form crescent. Place crescents seam side down 2 inches apart on baking sheet. Repeat with remaining dough, making 12 crescents in all. Cover baking sheet very loosely with plastic wrap and let rolls rise in warm place until almost double in size, about 35 minutes.

4 Preheat oven to 375°F. Remove plastic wrap; gently brush tops of rolls with beaten egg. Sprinkle half of rolls with sesame seeds and half with poppy seeds. Bake until rolls are golden brown, about 15 minutes. Remove from baking sheet and cool on rack. Serve warm or at room temperature.

Per serving (1 roll): 112 Cal, 1 g Fat, 0 g Sat Fat, 0 g Trans Fat, 0 mg Chol, 249 mg Sod, 22 g Carb, 2 g Fib, 4 g Prot, 11 mg Calc. ***POINTS*** value: ***2.***

MAKE AHEAD

To make these rolls up to 1 month ahead, wrap cooled rolls in heavy-duty foil and freeze. To serve, unwrap rolls, place on ungreased baking sheet, and bake in 450°F oven until soft and heated through, about 5 minutes.

Lemon-Strawberry Cream Roulade

prep 45 MIN bake 10 MIN serves 12 level ADVANCED

- ♦ 5 **large eggs**
- 1/2 **cup granulated sugar**
- 1 **teaspoon pure lemon extract**
- 1/2 **cup all-purpose flour**
- 1/3 **cup + 3 tablespoons confectioners' sugar**
- 1/4 **pound light cream cheese (Neufchâtel)**
- ♦ 1/2 **cup fat-free ricotta cheese**
- 1 1/2 **teaspoons grated lemon zest**
- ♦ 1 **(1-pound) container strawberries**
- 1/3 **cup no-sugar-added strawberry preserves**

1 Preheat oven to 350°F. Spray 15 x 10 x 1-inch jelly-roll pan with nonstick spray. Line with wax paper and spray paper with nonstick spray.

2 Separate eggs; put whites in large bowl and yolks in medium bowl. Beat whites with electric mixer on medium-high speed until soft peaks form. With mixer on high speed, gradually add 1/4 cup granulated sugar, beating until stiff peaks form. Set aside. Add extract and remaining 1/4 cup granulated sugar to yolks; beat with electric mixer on high speed until pale yellow, about 4 minutes. Fold in flour with rubber spatula. Pour yolk mixture over egg whites; gently fold together just until no white streaks remain. Scrape batter into pan and spread evenly. Bake until top springs back when pressed lightly with your fingertip, 12–15 minutes.

3 While cake bakes, sift 2 tablespoons confectioners' sugar onto clean kitchen towel. When cake is done, immediately invert onto towel. Carefully peel off wax paper from bottom of cake and discard. Starting from a long side, roll cake jelly-roll–style in towel. Cool rolled cake on rack. Meanwhile, beat cream cheese, ricotta, lemon zest, and 1/3 cup confectioners' sugar in small bowl until very smooth. Cover and refrigerate. Hull and slice 1 cup strawberries.

4 Unroll cake. Spread preserves over cake, leaving 1/2 inch border along farther long side. Arrange sliced strawberries over closer half of cake. Spread cake with ricotta mixture, leaving 1-inch border on one long side. Roll cake, starting from closer long side. Trim ends and place cake on platter. Sift remaining 1 tablespoon confectioners' sugar over cake and arrange whole strawberries around it. To serve, cut cake on slight diagonal into 12 slices with serrated knife.

Per serving (1 slice cake and 1 strawberry): 145 Cal, 4 g Fat, 2 g Sat Fat, 0 g Trans Fat, 97 mg Chol, 75 mg Sod, 22 g Carb, 1 g Fib, 5 g Prot, 40 mg Calc. ***POINTS*** value: ***3.***

MAKE AHEAD

The cake can be assembled up to 4 hours ahead. Cover tightly with plastic wrap and refrigerate. Dust the top with confectioners' sugar just before serving.

A Very Special Rosh Hashanah

BRANDIED MUSHROOM-BARLEY SOUP AND ROASTED BEET AND LATE-SUMMER FRUIT SALAD, PAGE 188

Brandied Mushroom-Barley Soup

prep 15 MIN cook 50 MIN serves 6 level BASIC

- ♦ 1 (1/2-ounce) package dried porcini mushrooms
- 2 cups boiling water
- 4 teaspoons olive oil
- ♦ 2 carrots, chopped
- ♦ 1 onion, chopped
- 1/2 teaspoon dried thyme
- ♦ 1/2 pound button mushrooms, sliced
- ♦ 1/2 pound shiitake mushrooms, stems discarded and caps sliced
- ♦ 1/2 pound oyster mushrooms, sliced
- 3 garlic cloves, minced
- 1/4 cup brandy or apple juice
- ♦ 6 cups reduced-sodium fat-free chicken broth
- ♦ 1/2 cup quick-cooking barley
- 1/4 teaspoon salt
- 1/4 teaspoon black pepper

1 Combine porcini mushrooms and water in medium bowl and let stand 20 minutes. Drain well and chop coarsely. Set aside.

2 Heat oil in nonstick Dutch oven over medium-high heat. Add carrots, onion, and thyme; cook, stirring occasionally, until vegetables begin to soften, 2–3 minutes. Stir in button, shiitake, and oyster mushrooms, garlic, and reserved porcini mushrooms; cook, stirring occasionally, until mushrooms are lightly browned, about 15 minutes. Remove Dutch oven from heat and carefully stir in brandy; return to heat and cook until almost absorbed, about 30 seconds.

3 Stir in broth and bring to boil. Reduce heat to medium, cover, and simmer 15 minutes. Stir in barley, salt, and pepper; continue to cook, covered, until barley is tender, 18–20 minutes.

Per serving (1 1/3 cups): 179 Cal, 5 g Fat, 1 g Sat Fat, 0 g Trans Fat, 4 mg Chol, 226 mg Sod, 26 g Carb, 6 g Fib, 10 g Prot, 44 mg Calc. ***POINTS*** value: ***3.***

IN THE KITCHEN

If you can't find oyster mushrooms at your market, substitute another wild mushroom, such as hen-of-the-woods or chanterelles, or simply double the amount of shiitakes in the recipe.

Roasted Beet and Late-Summer Fruit Salad

A Very Special Rosh Hashanah
MENU FOR SIX

3 DAYS AHEAD

- ☐ Make Brandied Mushroom-Barley Soup; let cool and refrigerate.

2 DAYS AHEAD

- ☐ Roast beets and make dressing for Roasted Beet and Late-Summer Fruit Salad; refrigerate separately.
- ☐ Bake Sweet Potato Tzimmes with Carrots and Prunes; cover pan with foil and refrigerate.

1 DAY AHEAD

- ☐ Bake Cinnamon-Apple Cake with Honey Glaze; let cool, wrap in plastic wrap, and store at room temperature. Glaze with honey and slice just before serving.
- ☐ Make Israeli Couscous Pilaf with Saffron; let cool and refrigerate.
- ☐ Make Roasted Kale with Caramelized Onions and Garlic; let cool and refrigerate.

2 HOURS AHEAD

- ☐ Make Apricot-Glazed Turkey Breast.

30 MINUTES AHEAD

- ☐ Reheat tzimmes in 300°F oven.

LAST MINUTE

- ☐ Reheat soup.
- ☐ Finish making salad.
- ☐ Reheat couscous.
- ☐ Reheat kale.
- ☐ Carve turkey breast.

prep 20 MIN roast 1 HR 5 MIN serves 6 level BASIC

- ♦ **1 pound beets, trimmed**
- **3 tablespoons orange juice**
- **1 small shallot, finely chopped**
- **1 tablespoon white-wine vinegar**
- **1 teaspoon Dijon mustard**
- **1/2 teaspoon salt**
- **1/8 teaspoon black pepper**
- **2 teaspoons olive oil**
- **1 teaspoon water**
- ♦ **2 peaches, halved, pitted, and cut into thin wedges**
- ♦ **2 large black plums, halved, pitted, and cut into thin wedges**
- ♦ **8 cups mixed baby greens**
- **3 tablespoons chopped toasted walnuts**

1 Preheat oven to 425°F.

2 Wrap beets in large sheet of foil and place on baking sheet. Roast until easily pierced with paring knife, about 1 hr 5 minutes. Let cool in foil 1 hour. Peel beets and cut into wedges.

3 Make dressing by combining orange juice, shallot, vinegar, mustard, salt, and pepper in medium bowl. Whisk in oil and water.

4 Combine beets, peaches, and plums in large bowl and toss with 4 tablespoons dressing. In separate bowl, toss greens with remaining dressing. Arrange beet mixture around edges of 6 salad plates. Divide greens evenly among plates, mounding them in center of each. Sprinkle plates evenly with walnuts.

Per serving (1 1/3 cups greens, 1/3 cup beets and fruit, and 1 1/2 teaspoons walnuts): 113 Cal, 4 g Fat, 1 g Sat Fat, 0 g Trans Fat, 0 mg Chol, 290 mg Sod, 18 g Carb, 4 g Fib, 4 g Prot, 60 mg Calc. ***POINTS*** value: ***2.***

IN THE KITCHEN

To keep your hands from getting stained while peeling and cutting the beets, wear rubber gloves.

Apricot-Glazed Turkey Breast

prep 25 MIN roast 1 HR 35 MIN serves 8 level BASIC

- **1 teaspoon ground cumin**
- **1 teaspoon paprika**
- **1/2 teaspoon ground ginger**
- **1 teaspoon salt**
- **1/2 teaspoon black pepper**
- ♦ **1 (4-pound) turkey breast, skin removed**
- **2 teaspoons olive oil**
- **2 cups water**
- **1/2 cup apricot preserves**
- **2 tablespoons honey**
- **2 tablespoons apple cider vinegar**
- **1 tablespoon Dijon mustard**

1 Preheat oven to 350°F. Spray rack with nonstick spray and set in roasting pan.

2 Combine cumin, paprika, ginger, salt, and pepper in small bowl. Rub turkey all over with oil; rub with cumin mixture. Place on rack and pour water into roasting pan. Roast until instant-read thermometer inserted into thickest part of breast registers 140°F, about 1 hour 15 minutes.

3 Meanwhile, combine preserves, honey, vinegar, and mustard in small saucepan set over medium-high heat. Bring to boil; cook, stirring, until mixture is smooth, about 1 minute. Remove from heat.

4 When turkey reaches 140°F, remove from oven and brush with one third of apricot glaze. Return to oven and roast 10 minutes longer. Brush again with one third of glaze, return to oven, and roast 5 minutes longer. Brush with remaining glaze and continue to roast until instant-read thermometer inserted into thickest part of breast registers 170°F, 5–10 minutes longer. Let stand 10 minutes; carve into 24 thin slices.

Per serving (3 slices): 271 Cal, 3 g Fat, 1 g Sat Fat, 0 g Trans Fat, 118 mg Chol, 421 mg Sod, 18 g Carb, 1 g Fib, 43 g Prot, 28 mg Calc. ***POINTS*** value: ***5.***

Israeli Couscous Pilaf with Saffron

prep 15 MIN cook 25 MIN serves 6 level BASIC

- 2 teaspoons olive oil
- ♦ 1 onion, finely chopped
- ♦ 1 small green bell pepper, finely chopped
- ♦ 1 celery stalk, finely chopped
- 2 garlic cloves, finely chopped
- 1 (8.8-ounce) package Israeli couscous
- 1 teaspoon ground coriander
- 1/4 teaspoon saffron threads, lightly crushed
- 2 cups water
- 1/2 teaspoon salt
- 1/4 teaspoon black pepper

1 Heat oil in large saucepan over medium-high heat. Add onion, bell pepper, and celery; cook, stirring occasionally, until onion begins to brown, 4–5 minutes. Stir in garlic and cook until fragrant, about 30 seconds.

2 Add couscous and cook until lightly toasted, about 1 minute. Stir in coriander and saffron. Add water, salt, and pepper; bring to boil. Reduce heat to medium low, cover, and simmer until liquid is absorbed and couscous is tender, 8–10 minutes.

Per serving (generous 1/2 cup): 190 Cal, 2 g Fat, 0 g Sat Fat, 0 g Trans Fat, 0 mg Chol, 204 mg Sod, 37 g Carb, 1 g Fib, 6 g Prot, 15 mg Calc. ***POINTS*** value: ***4.***

IN THE KITCHEN

Israeli couscous, also known as pearl couscous, has much larger grains than the fine North African couscous. The 8.8 ounces called for in this recipe is equal to 1 3/4 cups.

Sweet Potato Tzimmes with Carrots and Prunes

prep 20 MIN bake 1 HR 30 MIN serves 12 level BASIC

- ♦ **1½ pounds sweet potatoes, peeled and cut into ¾-inch chunks**
- ♦ **1 pound carrots, cut into ¾-inch pieces**
- **1 cup pitted prunes, halved**
- **½ cup golden raisins**
- **½ cup apple cider**
- **3 tablespoons packed dark brown sugar**
- **½ teaspoon salt**
- **⅛ teaspoon ground allspice**
- **1 tablespoon margarine, cut into small pieces**

1 Preheat oven to 375°F. Spray 11 x 7-inch baking dish with canola oil nonstick spray.

2 Combine sweet potatoes, carrots, prunes, raisins, cider, brown sugar, salt, and allspice in large bowl. Pour mixture into prepared baking dish and dot with margarine. Cover with foil and bake 30 minutes. Remove from oven; stir, cover again with foil, and bake 30 minutes longer. Remove from oven; stir again, cover, and bake until potatoes and carrots are very tender, about 30 minutes longer.

3 Let cool slightly; cut into 12 squares. (Tzimmes can be reheated in the pan, covered with foil, in a 300°F oven until hot, 20–30 minutes.)

Per serving (1 square): 135 Cal, 1 g Fat, 0 g Sat Fat, 0 g Trans Fat, 0 mg Chol, 134 mg Sod, 31 g Carb, 3 g Fib, 2 g Prot, 33 mg Calc. ***POINTS*** value: ***2.***

CHANGE IT UP

For Moroccan-style tzimmes, substitute orange juice for the cider and pitted dates for the prunes. The *POINTS* value will remain the same.

Roasted Kale with Caramelized Onions and Garlic

prep 20 MIN roast 25 MIN serves 6 level BASIC

- ♦ **2 (3/4-pound) bunches kale, tough stems removed and discarded, leaves thinly sliced**
- **4 teaspoons olive oil**
- **1/2 teaspoon salt**
- **1/4 teaspoon black pepper**
- ♦ **1 large onion, thinly sliced**
- **4 garlic cloves, thinly sliced**
- **1/4 teaspoon dried thyme**
- **2 teaspoons balsamic vinegar**

1 Preheat oven to 450°F. Spray large baking sheet with nonstick spray.

2 Toss kale in large bowl with 2 teaspoons oil, 1/4 teaspoon salt, and 1/8 teaspoon pepper. Transfer to baking sheet and roast, stirring once halfway through cooking time, until edges of kale begin to brown, about 10 minutes.

3 Meanwhile, heat remaining 2 teaspoons oil in large nonstick skillet over medium heat. Add onion, garlic, thyme, and remaining 1/4 teaspoon salt and 1/8 teaspoon pepper. Cook, stirring occasionally, until onions are golden, 20–25 minutes. Stir in vinegar and cook 1 minute. Add kale and cook, stirring, until hot, about 1 minute longer.

Per serving (1 cup): 73 Cal, 4 g Fat, 1 g Sat Fat, 0 g Trans Fat, 0 mg Chol, 223 mg Sod, 10 g Carb, 3 g Fib, 3 g Prot, 97 mg Calc. ***POINTS*** value: ***1.***

This recipe works with the Simply Filling technique.

Cinnamon-Apple Cake with Honey Glaze

prep 25 MIN bake 45 MIN serves 20 level INTERMEDIATE

- 3 cups all-purpose flour
- 1 1/2 cups packed light brown sugar
- 2 teaspoons baking powder
- 1/2 teaspoon baking soda
- 1 teaspoon cinnamon
- 1/2 teaspoon ground nutmeg
- 1/4 teaspoon salt
- ♦ 3 large eggs
- 3/4 cup apple cider
- 6 tablespoons canola oil
- 1 teaspoon vanilla extract
- ♦ 2 large Golden Delicious apples, peeled, cored, and chopped
- 1/4 cup honey, warmed

1 Preheat oven to 375°F. Spray 10-inch tube pan with nonstick spray and dust with flour.

2 Whisk together flour, brown sugar, baking powder, baking soda, cinnamon, nutmeg, and salt in large bowl. Whisk together eggs, cider, oil, and vanilla in medium bowl. Add egg mixture to flour mixture and beat with electric mixer on low speed until well combined, about 3 minutes. Stir in apples.

3 Pour batter into pan. Bake until toothpick inserted into center of cake comes out clean, about 45 minutes. Cool in pan on rack 15 minutes. Remove cake from pan and cool completely on rack. Drizzle with honey just before serving and cut into 20 slices.

Per serving (1 slice): 206 Cal, 6 g Fat, 1 g Sat Fat, 0 g Trans Fat, 32 mg Chol, 116 mg Sod, 38 g Carb, 1 g Fib, 3 g Prot, 31 mg Calc. ***POINTS*** value: ***4.***

CHANGE IT UP

To make a spiced pear cake, use pumpkin-pie spice instead of the cinnamon and nutmeg, and substitute fresh pears for the apples. The *POINTS* value will remain the same.

A Traditional Thanksgiving

Autumn Salad with Pears and Pomegranate

prep 20 MIN cook NONE serves 12 level BASIC

- ♦ 2 heads Bibb or Boston lettuce, cut into bite-size pieces
- ♦ 1 head radicchio, thinly sliced
- ♦ 2 Asian pears, cored and thinly sliced
- ♦ 1 fennel bulb, halved and thinly sliced, feathery fronds chopped
- ♦ 1/2 cup tender celery leaves
- 1/4 cup unseasoned rice vinegar
- 2 tablespoons flaxseed oil or canola oil
- 2 teaspoons honey
- 1 1/2 teaspoons salt
- 1/2 teaspoon black pepper
- ♦ 1/2 cup pomegranate seeds

Combine lettuce, radicchio, pears, fennel bulb and fronds, and celery leaves in large bowl. Whisk together vinegar, oil, honey, salt, and pepper in small bowl. Just before serving, drizzle vinaigrette over salad and toss. Sprinkle with pomegranate seeds.

Per serving (1 1/4 cups): 54 Cal, 3 g Fat, 0 g Sat Fat, 0 g Trans Fat, 0 mg Chol, 301 mg Sod, 8 g Carb, 2 g Fib, 1 g Prot, 18 mg Calc. ***POINTS*** value: ***1.***

A Traditional Thanksgiving

MENU FOR TWELVE

3 DAYS AHEAD

- ☐ Begin thawing turkey in refrigerator if frozen.
- ☐ Make Spiced Cranberry Sauce.

2 DAYS AHEAD

- ☐ Make vinaigrette for Autumn Salad with Pears and Pomegranate; refrigerate.
- ☐ Prepare but do not bake Apple-Celery Stuffing; refrigerate.
- ☐ Make Creamy Mashed Sweet Potatoes but do not reheat; refrigerate.

1 DAY AHEAD

- ☐ Make brine for Brown Sugar–Brined Turkey with Golden Gravy; put turkey in brine last thing at night or first thing the following morning.
- ☐ Make Pumpkin and Ricotta Cheesecake.
- ☐ Cook, drain, and cool beans for Green Beans with Mushrooms and Hazelnuts; wrap in paper towels and then in plastic wrap and refrigerate.

4 HOURS AHEAD

- ☐ Remove turkey from brine and prepare for roasting; stuff if desired.

3 HOURS AHEAD

- ☐ Begin roasting turkey.

LAST MINUTE

- ☐ Assemble salad.
- ☐ Finish making green beans.
- ☐ Reheat sweet potatoes.
- ☐ Make gravy and carve turkey.

Brown Sugar–Brined Turkey with Golden Gravy

prep 30 MIN roast/cook 3 HRS serves 12 WITH LEFTOVERS level INTERMEDIATE

- **1 cup packed light brown sugar**
- **3/4 cup kosher salt**
- **5 bay leaves**
- **8 cups boiling water**
- ♦ **1 (12-pound) turkey, giblets reserved for another use**
- **Apple-Celery Stuffing (optional; see page 198)**
- **2 teaspoons canola oil**
- **1/2 teaspoon fine sea salt**
- **3/4 teaspoon black pepper**
- ♦ **1 3/4 cups reduced-sodium chicken broth**
- **2 tablespoons all-purpose flour**

1 Combine brown sugar, kosher salt, bay leaves, and boiling water in 5-gallon pot and stir until sugar and salt are dissolved. Let cool to room temperature; add turkey and enough cold water to just cover turkey. Refrigerate for at least 4 hours or up to overnight.

2 Place oven rack in bottom third of oven. Preheat oven to 450°F. Remove turkey from brine, rinse under cold water, and place in roasting pan fitted with roasting rack. Pat dry inside and out with paper towels. Tuck wing tips under bird. Spoon stuffing (if using) into cavity of turkey, filling it no more than two thirds full. Tie turkey legs together with kitchen string. Rub skin with oil and sprinkle with sea salt and pepper. Pour 3/4 cup broth into bottom of pan; roast turkey 20 minutes. Reduce oven temperature to 350°F. Roast until instant-read thermometer inserted into thickest part of thigh registers 180°F, about 2 hours 30 minutes longer. (During last half hour of cooking, bake any leftover stuffing in buttered baking dish alongside turkey.) Transfer turkey to platter and let stand 30 minutes.

3 To make gravy, pour drippings and juices from roasting pan into gravy separator or glass measuring cup. Spoon 1 1/2 tablespoons of fat into small saucepan; discard remaining fat. Place saucepan over medium heat. Stir in flour; cook, stirring, 2 minutes. Add remaining broth to pan juices to yield 1 1/2 cups in all; whisk broth mixture into flour mixture. Cook, stirring frequently, until gravy is thickened, 4–5 minutes.

4 Discard turkey skin; carve breast and thigh meat into 24 slices; save drumsticks and wings for another use. Serve turkey slices with gravy and stuffing.

Per serving (2 slices turkey without skin and 2 tablespoons gravy): 194 Cal, 4 g Fat, 1 g Sat Fat, 0 g Trans Fat, 114 mg Chol, 484 mg Sod, 2 g Carb, 0 g Fib, 34 g Prot, 26 mg Calc. ***POINTS*** value: ***4.***

IN THE KITCHEN

Roasting a 12-pound turkey will yield a good 2 pounds of skinless sliced white meat (from the breast) and 1 pound of skinless sliced dark meat (from the thighs). You'll also have leftover drumsticks, wings, and lots of scraps from the carcass to use in soup, stock, salads, and sandwiches.

BROWN SUGAR–BRINED TURKEY WITH GOLDEN GRAVY

Apple-Celery Stuffing

prep 20 MIN bake/cook 30 MIN serves 12 level BASIC

- **12 slices (1/2 pound) reduced-calorie whole-grain sandwich bread, diced**
- **1 tablespoon olive oil**
- **1 tablespoon unsalted butter**
- ♦ **5 celery stalks, thinly sliced**
- ♦ **3 Gala apples, cored and diced**
- ♦ **1 large red onion, diced**
- **1/2 teaspoon salt**
- **1 teaspoon black pepper**
- **1/2 cup chopped fresh parsley leaves**
- **1 3/4 teaspoons dried rubbed sage**
- ♦ **2 cups reduced-sodium chicken broth**

1 Preheat oven to 250°F. Place bread on baking sheet and bake until dried, about 20 minutes. Transfer to large bowl.

2 Heat oil and butter in large skillet over medium-high heat until butter is melted. Add celery, apples, onion, salt, and pepper; cook, stirring frequently, until apples are softened, 7–8 minutes. Add to bowl with bread along with parsley and sage; toss to combine. Add broth and toss again. Let cool.

3 Spoon stuffing loosely into turkey. This recipe makes about 9 cups, enough to stuff a turkey up to 16 pounds; any extra stuffing can be baked in buttered baking dish alongside turkey until browned and crisp on top.

Per serving (3/4 cup): 92 Cal, 3 g Fat, 1 g Sat Fat, 0 g Trans Fat, 3 mg Chol, 234 mg Sod, 16 g Carb, 4 g Fib, 3 g Prot, 37 mg Calc. ***POINTS*** value: ***1.***

IN THE KITCHEN

If you'd rather bake the stuffing separately, transfer it to a buttered 9 x 13-inch baking dish and bake at 350°F until crisp on top, about 30 minutes.

Green Beans with Mushrooms and Hazelnuts

prep 20 MIN cook 30 MIN serves 12 level BASIC

- ♦ 3 **pounds green beans, trimmed**
- 1 **tablespoon olive oil**
- 2 **shallots, halved and thinly sliced**
- ♦ 1 **(10-ounce) package sliced cremini mushrooms**
- 2 **tablespoons balsamic vinegar**
- 1/2 **teaspoon salt**
- 1/4 **teaspoon black pepper**
- 1/3 **cup toasted hazelnuts, chopped**

1 Bring large pot of water to boil; add beans and cook just until bright green and tender, about 5 minutes. Drain, cool under cold running water, and drain again.

2 Heat oil over medium heat in very large skillet. Add shallots and cook, stirring, until softened, about 3 minutes. Add mushrooms and cook until liquid evaporates and mushrooms begin to brown, about 6 minutes. Add beans, vinegar, salt, and pepper; toss until beans are hot, about 2 minutes. Transfer to serving dish and sprinkle with hazelnuts.

Per serving (1 cup): 79 Cal, 3 g Fat, 0 g Sat Fat, 0 g Trans Fat, 0 mg Chol, 102 mg Sod, 11 g Carb, 4 g Fib, 3 g Prot, 58 mg Calc. ***POINTS*** value: ***1.***

Creamy Mashed Sweet Potatoes

prep 15 MIN cook 25 MIN serves 12 level BASIC

- ♦ **5 sweet potatoes, peeled and quartered**
- **1/2 cup low-fat buttermilk**
- **1/4 cup fat-free half-and-half, warmed**
- **1 tablespoon unsalted butter**
- **1/2 teaspoon cinnamon**
- **1 teaspoon salt**
- **2 tablespoons packed light brown sugar**

1 Put potatoes in large saucepan and cover with cold water; bring to boil over high heat. Reduce heat and simmer until potatoes are tender and almost falling apart, about 20 minutes.

2 Drain potatoes and return them to pan. Mash with potato masher or whip with handheld mixer until smooth. Stir in buttermilk, half-and-half, butter, cinnamon, salt, and 1 tablespoon brown sugar.

3 Reheat on stove over medium heat if necessary, adding a little water if mash is too thick. Transfer to serving bowl and sprinkle with remaining 1 tablespoon brown sugar.

Per serving (1/2 cup): 91 Cal, 1 g Fat, 1 g Sat Fat, 0 g Trans Fat, 3 mg Chol, 218 mg Sod, 19 g Carb, 1 g Fib, 2 g Prot, 35 mg Calc. ***POINTS*** value: **2.**

CHANGE IT UP

If sweet potatoes topped with marshmallows are a must at your holiday table, transfer this mash to an ovenproof casserole dish, sprinkle with mini-marshmallows, and broil until the marshmallows are melted and lightly browned. One third of a cup of mini-marshmallows with each serving will increase the per-serving *POINTS* value by *1.*

Spiced Cranberry Sauce

prep 10 MIN cook 15 MIN serves 24 level BASIC

- **1½ cups cranberry juice cocktail**
- **¾ cup dried apricots, chopped**
- ♦ **2 (12-ounce) bags fresh or frozen cranberries**
- **1¼ cups sugar**
- **2 tablespoons minced peeled fresh ginger**
- **1 cinnamon stick**

1 In large saucepan, combine cranberry juice and apricots; let stand 10 minutes to allow apricots to soften. Stir in cranberries, sugar, ginger, and cinnamon stick and bring to boil over high heat. Reduce heat to medium; simmer until most cranberries pop open and sauce thickens, about 10 minutes.

2 Pour sauce into medium bowl and let cool. Remove and discard cinnamon stick. Cover sauce and refrigerate until cold, at least 3 hours. This dish can be made up to 3 days ahead.

Per serving (3 tablespoons): 79 Cal, 0 g Fat, 0 g Sat Fat, 0 g Trans Fat, 0 mg Chol, 1 mg Sod, 20 g Carb, 1 g Fib, 0 g Prot, 3 mg Calc. ***POINTS*** value: ***1.***

♦ FILLING EXTRA
Add a chopped apple to the sauce along with the cranberries.

PUMPKIN AND RICOTTA CHEESECAKE

Pumpkin and Ricotta Cheesecake

prep 25 MIN bake 1 HR 20 MIN serves 12 level INTERMEDIATE

18 gingersnaps, broken in half
2 tablespoons unsalted butter, melted
1/2 cup + 2 tablespoons granulated sugar
♦ **1 (15-ounce) container fat-free ricotta cheese**
1 (8-ounce) package light cream cheese (Neufchâtel)
1/2 cup packed light brown sugar
2 tablespoons cornstarch
1 1/2 teaspoons cinnamon
1/2 teaspoon ground ginger
1/4 teaspoon grated nutmeg, plus more for garnish
♦ **1 (15-ounce) can pumpkin puree**
♦ **1 cup fat-free egg substitute**
1 cup thawed frozen fat-free whipped topping

1 Preheat oven to 350°F. Put gingersnaps in food processor and pulse to make fine crumbs. Add melted butter and 2 tablespoons granulated sugar; pulse until blended. Spoon crumb mixture into 9-inch springform pan; press evenly onto bottom and up sides of pan. Bake until dried, about 8 minutes. Let cool.

2 Put ricotta in food processor (bowl need not be washed out first) and pulse until smooth. Add cream cheese, brown sugar, cornstarch, cinnamon, ginger, nutmeg, and remaining 1/2 cup granulated sugar; process until blended and smooth, stopping to scrape down sides of bowl a few times. Add pumpkin puree and egg substitute; pulse until mixed. Pour filling over crust and level top. Bake until filling is set and no longer jiggles in center, about 1 hour 10 minutes.

3 Cool cheesecake in pan on rack. Cover pan with plastic wrap; refrigerate until chilled, 4 hours or overnight. To serve, release and remove sides of pan. Spread top of cheesecake evenly with whipped topping and sprinkle with nutmeg. Cut into 12 slices.

Per serving (1 slice): 254 Cal, 8 g Fat, 4 g Sat Fat, 0 g Trans Fat, 25 mg Chol, 236 mg Sod, 38 g Carb, 2 g Fib, 8 g Prot, 114 mg Calc. ***POINTS*** value: ***5.***

IN THE KITCHEN

The top of the cheesecake will crack as it bakes and cools. The tart can be baked up to 2 days ahead and kept refrigerated.

Elegant Christmas Table

Sugar-and-Spice Cider Punch

prep 5 MIN cook 5 MIN serves 12 level BASIC

7 cups apple cider
1 cup pure cherry juice
2 tablespoons packed light brown sugar
2 strips orange peel, removed with a vegetable peeler
2 cinnamon sticks
8 whole cloves
1 large star anise pod
Brandy (optional)

Combine cider, cherry juice, and brown sugar in large saucepan. Tie orange peel, cinnamon sticks, cloves, and star anise together in small square of cheesecloth and add to pan. Set over medium heat and cook, stirring occasionally, just until bubbles form around edges, about 5 minutes. Reduce heat to low and continue to cook to let flavors infuse, about 2 minutes. Discard spices; ladle punch into small cups and add splash of brandy (if using).

Per serving (2/3 cup without brandy): 91 Cal, 0 g Fat, 0 g Sat Fat, 0 g Trans Fat, 0 mg Chol, 18 mg Sod, 23 g Carb, 0 g Fib, 0 g Prot, 2 mg Calc. ***POINTS*** value: ***2.***

IN THE KITCHEN
Be sure to use only 100 percent pure fruit juice with no added sweeteners, such as cane sugar or high fructose corn syrup, in this punch.

Elegant Christmas Table
MENU FOR TWELVE

2 DAYS AHEAD
- ☐ Make spread for Smoked Trout Canapés; refrigerate. Toast bread for canapés; let cool and store in airtight container.
- ☐ Make dressing for Spinach-Apple Salad with Blue Cheese and Pecans; refrigerate.

1 DAY AHEAD
- ☐ Bake Pear-Cranberry Linzer Tart; store at room temperature.
- ☐ Make cider glaze and pilaf for Crown Roast of Pork with Cider Glaze and Mixed-Grain Pilaf; refrigerate separately.

2 HOURS AHEAD
- ☐ Begin roasting crown roast of pork; reheat pilaf briefly in microwave before stuffing roast.
- ☐ Prepare Roast Carrots and Brussels Sprouts with Shallots and Sherry Vinegar but do not roast; cover pan with foil and set aside at room temperature.
- ☐ Make Parsnip and Potato Puree; refrigerate.

1 HOUR AHEAD
- ☐ Assemble canapés.

30 MINUTES AHEAD
- ☐ Roast carrots and Brussels sprouts.
- ☐ Make Sugar-and-Spice Cider Punch.

LAST MINUTE
- ☐ Finish making spinach-apple salad.
- ☐ Reheat parsnip puree.

Smoked Trout Canapés

prep 15 MIN   bake 10 MIN   serves 12   level BASIC

- 3 ounces light cream cheese (Neufchâtel)
- ♦ 1/2 cup plain fat-free Greek yogurt
- ♦ 3 ounces skinless smoked trout fillet, broken into pieces
- 2 tablespoons chopped fresh dill
- 1/8 teaspoon black pepper
- ♦ 2 tablespoons minced red onion
- 18 slices cocktail pumpernickel or rye bread
- Small dill sprigs, for garnish

1 Combine cream cheese and yogurt in food processor and pulse until blended. Add trout, chopped dill, pepper, and 1 tablespoon onion; pulse until blended. Scrape spread into small bowl, cover, and refrigerate at least 2 hours to allow flavors to blend.

2 Preheat oven to 350°F. Arrange pumpernickel on baking sheet. Bake until lightly toasted but not dry, about 8 minutes. Let cool.

3 Spread each piece of toast with 1 tablespoon spread; sprinkle evenly with remaining 1 tablespoon onion and cut each in half diagonally. Garnish with dill sprigs.

Per serving (3 canapés): 93 Cal, 3 g Fat, 1 g Sat Fat, 0 g Trans Fat, 11 mg Chol, 379 mg Sod, 12 g Carb, 2 g Fib, 7 g Prot, 32 mg Calc. ***POINTS*** value: ***2.***

Spinach-Apple Salad with Blue Cheese and Pecans

prep 20 MIN cook NONE serves 12 level BASIC

- 1 shallot, minced
- 2 tablespoons lemon juice
- 1 tablespoon olive oil
- 1 tablespoon red-wine vinegar
- 1 teaspoon Dijon mustard
- 1/2 teaspoon salt
- 1/4 teaspoon black pepper
- ♦ 2 (6-ounce) bags baby spinach leaves
- ♦ 3 apples, cored and thinly sliced
- 2/3 cup tart dried cherries
- 1/2 cup crumbled reduced-fat blue cheese
- 1/3 cup pecans, toasted and coarsely chopped

1 In small bowl, whisk together shallot, lemon juice, oil, vinegar, mustard, salt, and pepper until well blended.

2 Put spinach, apples, cherries, and blue cheese in large bowl. Pour dressing over salad and toss to coat. Divide evenly among 12 salad plates and sprinkle evenly with pecans.

Per serving (1 2/3 cups): 95 Cal, 4 g Fat, 1 g Sat Fat, 0 g Trans Fat, 1 mg Chol, 175 mg Sod, 15 g Carb, 3 g Fib, 2 g Prot, 38 mg Calc. ***POINTS*** value: ***2.***

CHANGE IT UP

For a Spinach-Pear Salad with Blue Cheese, replace the apples with 3 ripe red pears; use dried cranberries instead of cherries and walnuts instead of pecans; and omit the lemon juice and red-wine vinegar and instead use 3 tablespoons apple cider vinegar. The *POINTS* value will remain the same.

Crown Roast of Pork with Cider Glaze and Mixed-Grain Pilaf

prep 20 MIN cook/roast 2 HRS 5 MIN serves 12 level INTERMEDIATE

- **1½ cups apple cider**
- ♦ **12-rib crown roast of pork, trimmed and prepared by butcher (about 5½ pounds)**
- **1½ teaspoons kosher salt**
- **1 teaspoon black pepper**
- ♦ **3 cups reduced-sodium chicken broth**
- ♦ **1 small onion, chopped**
- **¼ teaspoon salt**
- ♦ **1 cup brown and wild rice blend**
- ♦ **½ cup pearl barley, rinsed**
- **⅔ cup dried cranberries**

1 Put cider in small saucepan and simmer over medium heat until reduced to ½ cup, about 20 minutes.

2 Preheat oven to 375°F. Line large roasting pan with foil; spray foil with nonstick spray. Sprinkle pork all over with kosher salt and pepper and place in pan (if necessary, fit small ovenproof bowl into center of roast to help keep its circular shape). Wrap tips of bones in foil to prevent burning. Roast pork for 1 hour 15 minutes, brushing it with cider glaze about every 20 minutes.

3 Meanwhile, to make pilaf, combine broth, onion, and salt in medium saucepan and bring to boil over high heat. Stir in rice blend and barley; return to boil. Reduce heat and simmer, covered, until liquid is absorbed and grains are tender, about 45 minutes. Add cranberries, cover, and set aside 10 minutes. Fluff with fork.

4 Remove pork from oven; remove bowl (if used). Mound pilaf in center of pork and return to oven; roast until instant-read thermometer inserted into pork without touching bone registers 160°F, 30–45 minutes longer.

5 Using 2 spatulas, transfer roast to platter; if any pilaf falls out, just replace it. Let roast rest 20 minutes; remove and discard foil tips and any string used to tie roast. Carve pork between ribs and serve each chop with a scoop of pilaf.

Per serving (1 chop and scant ½ cup pilaf): 318 Cal, 11 g Fat, 4 g Sat Fat, 0 g Trans Fat, 66 mg Chol, 558 mg Sod, 25 g Carb, 2 g Fib, 30 g Prot, 34 mg Calc. ***POINTS*** value: ***7.***

IN THE KITCHEN

Crown roasts usually need to be special ordered, so call or stop by your butcher or your supermarket's meat department several days ahead to make the necessary arrangements.

CROWN ROAST OF PORK WITH CIDER GLAZE AND MIXED-GRAIN PILAF

Parsnip and Potato Puree

prep 15 MIN cook 25 MIN serves 12 level BASIC

- ♦ **2 1/2 pounds parsnips (about 8), peeled and cut into 1-inch slices**
- ♦ **1 1/2 pounds Yukon Gold potatoes (about 4), peeled and cut into 1-inch cubes**
- **1/2 cup fat-free half-and-half, warmed**
- **1 teaspoon salt**
- **Pinch cayenne**

1 Put parsnips and potatoes in large pot and add enough water to cover by 1 inch; bring to boil over high heat. Reduce heat and simmer until vegetables are very tender, about 20 minutes.

2 Drain vegetables and pass them through food mill or mash with potato masher or large fork. Stir in half-and-half, salt, and cayenne. Reheat over low heat if necessary.

Per serving (1/2 cup): 134 Cal, 0 g Fat, 0 g Sat Fat, 0 g Trans Fat, 0 mg Chol, 215 mg Sod, 30 g Carb, 5 g Fib, 3 g Prot, 50 mg Calc. ***POINTS*** value: ***2.***

IN THE KITCHEN

You can substitute 1/2 cup of low-fat buttermilk for the half-and-half in this recipe if you like for no change in *POINTS* value.

Roast Carrots and Brussels Sprouts with Shallots and Sherry Vinegar

prep 20 MIN roast 20 MIN serves 12 level BASIC

- ♦ **1 (1-pound) bag peeled baby carrots, halved lengthwise**
- ♦ **2 pints Brussels sprouts, halved**
- **3 shallots, thickly sliced**
- **4 teaspoons olive oil**
- **1 1/4 teaspoons salt**
- **1/2 teaspoon black pepper**
- **1 1/2 tablespoons sherry vinegar or apple cider vinegar**

Preheat oven to 450°F. Place carrots, Brussels sprouts, and shallots on large baking sheet. Drizzle with oil, sprinkle with salt and pepper, and toss to coat. Roast until carrots are just tender and Brussels sprouts and shallots begin to brown, 20–25 minutes, stirring once halfway through cooking time. Toss with vinegar.

Per serving (scant 2/3 cup): 44 Cal, 2 g Fat, 0 g Sat Fat, 0 g Trans Fat, 0 mg Chol, 263 mg Sod, 7 g Carb, 2 g Fib, 1 g Prot, 23 mg Calc. ***POINTS*** value: ***1.***

This recipe works with the Simply Filling technique.

PEAR-CRANBERRY LINZER TART

Pear-Cranberry Linzer Tart

prep 30 MIN cook 50 MIN serves 16 level INTERMEDIATE

- **1 1/2 cups white whole wheat flour**
- **1 teaspoon baking powder**
- **1/2 teaspoon cinnamon**
- **1/3 cup toasted almonds**
- **5 tablespoons light stick butter**
- **3/4 cup packed light brown sugar**
- ♦ **2 large egg whites**
- **1/3 cup raspberry preserves**
- **1/2 cup dried cranberries**
- **1 tablespoon granulated sugar**
- **2 teaspoons cornstarch**
- ♦ **2 ripe large pears, cored and cut into 1/2-inch-thick slices**

1 Preheat oven to 350 F. Spray 10-inch removable-bottom tart pan with nonstick spray and dust with flour.

2 In medium bowl, whisk together flour, baking powder, and cinnamon. Put almonds in food processor and pulse until finely chopped; measure out 1 tablespoon almonds and set aside. Add butter and brown sugar to remaining almonds; pulse until blended. Add egg whites and pulse until blended. Add flour mixture and pulse until combined. Spoon mixture into tart pan and press evenly onto bottom of pan. Spread evenly with preserves, leaving a 1/2-inch border. Set aside 1 tablespoon cranberries and sprinkle remaining cranberries over preserves.

3 Mix granulated sugar and cornstarch together in cup. Place pears in medium bowl and sprinkle with cornstarch mixture; toss gently to combine. Arrange pear slices in pan in concentric circles. Sprinkle with reserved 1 tablespoon almonds and 1 tablespoon cranberries. Bake tart until toothpick inserted into center comes out with a few moist crumbs, about 50 minutes. Cool completely on wire rack. To serve, remove tart ring and cut tart into 16 slices.

Per serving (1 slice): 150 Cal, 4 g Fat, 1 g Sat Fat, 0 g Trans Fat, 6 mg Chol, 37 mg Sod, 29 g Carb, 2 g Fib, 3 g Prot, 26 mg Calc. ***POINTS*** value: ***3.***

IN THE KITCHEN
This tart can also be baked in a 10-inch springform pan.

Kwanzaa Dinner

African Peanut Soup

prep 15 MIN cook 30 MIN serves 8 level BASIC

- ♦ 2 green bell peppers, chopped
- ♦ 1 onion, chopped
- 1 tablespoon grated peeled fresh ginger
- 2 garlic cloves, minced
- ♦ 1 jalapeño pepper, seeded and minced
- ♦ 2 (32-ounce) cartons reduced-sodium chicken broth
- ♦ 1 (14½-ounce) can fire-roasted tomatoes
- ½ cup reduced-fat peanut butter
- ¼ teaspoon salt
- 1 teaspoon ground cardamom
- 3 tablespoons chopped fresh cilantro

1 Spray large nonstick saucepan with nonstick spray and set over medium heat. Add bell peppers, onion, ginger, garlic, and jalapeño; cook, stirring frequently, until vegetables are softened, about 6 minutes. Stir in broth, tomatoes, peanut butter, and salt; bring to boil. Reduce heat and simmer, covered, stirring occasionally, until vegetables are very soft, about 20 minutes.

2 Remove pan from heat; let mixture cool 5 minutes. Transfer in batches to food processor or blender and pulse until smooth. Return soup to pan; reheat if necessary. Stir in cardamom and cilantro.

Per serving (1 cup): 147 Cal, 7 g Fat, 2 g Sat Fat, 0 g Trans Fat, 5 mg Chol, 407 mg Sod, 14 g Carb, 2 g Fib, 9 g Prot, 43 mg Calc. ***POINTS*** value: ***3.***

IN THE KITCHEN

Use caution when blending hot liquids; their heat can cause the air in a blender to expand, sometimes enough to blow the lid off the blender and send scalding liquid all over your kitchen. To play it safe, never fill the container more than half full, place the lid on and hold it down gently with a folded kitchen towel, and start blending on low speed.

Kwanzaa Dinner

MENU FOR EIGHT

2 TO 3 DAYS AHEAD

- ☐ Prepare pie dough for Orange–Sweet Potato Pie; refrigerate.
- ☐ Make African Peanut Soup, leaving out cardamom and cilantro; let cool and refrigerate.

1 DAY AHEAD

- ☐ Make Rice and Pigeon Peas; let cool and refrigerate.
- ☐ Make Creamed Collards with Sweet Onions and Crispy Bacon; let cool and refrigerate collards and bacon separately.
- ☐ Bake sweet potato pie; let cool, cover, and store at room temperature.

1 HOUR AHEAD

- ☐ Make Sorghum-Glazed Ham.

LAST MINUTE

- ☐ Reheat soup; stir in cardamom and cilantro.
- ☐ Reheat collards; garnish with bacon.
- ☐ Reheat rice, adding 1–2 tablespoons water if needed.

Sorghum-Glazed Ham

prep 10 MIN bake 45 MIN serves 12 level BASIC

- **3/4 cup balsamic vinegar**
- **2 tablespoons sorghum syrup**
- **1 teaspoon Worcestershire sauce**
- **1 teaspoon unsalted butter**
- **2 teaspoons chopped fresh thyme**
- ♦ **1 (3-pound) low-sodium lean boneless ham**

1 Combine vinegar, syrup, and Worcestershire in small saucepan; bring to boil over medium-high heat. Boil until mixture is reduced and syrupy, about 10 minutes. Remove saucepan from heat; swirl in butter and thyme.

2 Meanwhile, preheat oven to 350°F. Line medium baking pan with foil and spray foil with nonstick spray. Place ham, cut side down, in pan. Spoon glaze over ham. Bake, uncovered, until ham is heated through and instant-read thermometer registers 140°F, about 30 minutes. Transfer to cutting board and cover loosely with foil. Let stand 10 minutes. Cut into 12 (1/2-inch-thick) slices.

Per serving (1 slice glazed ham): 158 Cal, 4 g Fat, 2 g Sat Fat, 0 g Trans Fat, 55 mg Chol, 846 mg Sod, 10 g Carb, 0 g Fib, 19 g Prot, 9 mg Calc. ***POINTS*** value: ***3.***

IN THE KITCHEN

Sorghum syrup is a traditional Southern sweetener with a rich amber color and mild caramel flavor. It comes from the cane of sorghum grass, a popular crop in Africa, and is believed to have been introduced to this country during the slave trade. Sorghum is available in supermarkets regionally, in natural foods stores, and from online sources. You can substitute 1 tablespoon honey and 1 tablespoon molasses for the sorghum in this recipe with good results.

SORGHUM-GLAZED HAM WITH RICE AND PIGEON PEAS, PAGE 218

Rice and Pigeon Peas

prep 15 MIN cook 45 MIN serves 8 level BASIC

- **2 teaspoons olive oil**
- ♦ **1 onion, thinly sliced**
- **2 garlic cloves, minced**
- ♦ **1 Scotch bonnet or other very hot pepper, seeded and minced**
- ♦ **1 3/4 cups brown basmati rice**
- ♦ **4 cups reduced-sodium chicken broth**
- **1/2 cup light coconut milk**
- ♦ **1 (15-ounce) can pigeon peas or black-eyed peas, rinsed and drained**

Heat oil in large saucepan over medium-high heat. Add onion, garlic, and pepper; cook, stirring often, until vegetables are softened, about 5 minutes. Add rice and stir to coat. Stir in broth and coconut milk; bring to boil. Reduce heat and simmer, covered, until liquid is absorbed and rice is tender, 45–50 minutes. Stir in peas and heat through.

Per serving (3/4 cup): 208 Cal, 4 g Fat, 2 g Sat Fat, 0 g Trans Fat, 2 mg Chol, 172 mg Sod, 38 g Carb, 3 g Fib, 7 g Prot, 21 mg Calc. ***POINTS*** value: ***4.***

IN THE KITCHEN

The oils from these super-spicy peppers like Scotch bonnet can burn your flesh, so be sure not to touch the peppers themselves. It's safest to wear disposable plastic gloves when seeding and chopping these peppers.

Creamed Collards with Sweet Onions and Crispy Bacon

prep 25 MIN cook 1 HR 10 MIN serves 8 level INTERMEDIATE

- **3 teaspoons olive oil**
- **2 tablespoons all-purpose flour**
- ♦ **2 cups fat-free milk**
- **1/4 teaspoon ground nutmeg**
- **1/2 teaspoon salt**
- **4 slices turkey bacon, coarsely chopped**
- ♦ **2 Vidalia or other sweet onions, thinly sliced**
- **4 garlic cloves, chopped**
- ♦ **2 large bunches collard greens, tough stems removed and discarded, leaves coarsely chopped (about 16 cups)**
- **1/2 cup water**
- **1/4 teaspoon salt**

1 To make sauce, heat 2 teaspoons oil in medium saucepan over medium-high heat. Add flour and cook, stirring constantly, 1 minute. Whisk in milk, nutmeg, and 1/4 teaspoon salt; bring to boil. Reduce heat and simmer, whisking occasionally, until mixture thickens, about 5 minutes. Remove saucepan from heat, cover, and set aside.

2 To make bacon, spray small nonstick skillet with nonstick spray and set over medium-high heat. Add bacon and cook, stirring frequently, until crisp, 3–4 minutes. Transfer to paper towels to drain.

3 To make collards, heat remaining 1 teaspoon oil in large nonstick skillet over medium-high heat. Add onions and garlic and cook, stirring occasionally, until soft, 6–8 minutes. Add collards to skillet a few handfuls at a time, stirring and allowing leaves to wilt slightly before adding more. Add water; bring to boil. Reduce heat and simmer, covered, until collards are softened, about 15 minutes.

4 Stir in sauce. Reduce heat and simmer, covered, stirring occasionally, until collards are fork-tender, 35–40 minutes. Remove from heat and sprinkle with bacon.

Per serving (3/4 cup): 91 Cal, 4 g Fat, 1 g Sat Fat, 0 g Trans Fat, 8 mg Chol, 341 mg Sod, 11 g Carb, 3 g Fib, 5 g Prot, 184 mg Calc. ***POINTS*** value: ***2.***

IN THE KITCHEN

Substitute any hearty winter green, such as kale or mustard greens, for the collards in this recipe.

ORANGE–SWEET POTATO PIE

Orange–Sweet Potato Pie

prep 25 MIN bake 1 HR 10 MIN serves 12 level INTERMEDIATE

- 1 cup all-purpose flour
- 1/4 cup whole wheat pastry flour
- 1 tablespoon granulated sugar
- 3/4 teaspoon salt
- 3 tablespoons canola oil
- 2–3 tablespoons water
- 1 (15 1/2-ounce) can cut sweet yams in light syrup, drained
- 3/4 cup packed dark brown sugar
- ♦ 1 (12-ounce) can fat-free evaporated milk
- 1/4 cup orange juice
- 2 tablespoons molasses or sorghum
- ♦ 2 large eggs
- ♦ 1 large egg white
- 1 1/2 teaspoons pumpkin-pie spice

1 To make crust, put all-purpose flour, pastry flour, sugar, and 1/4 teaspoon salt in food processor; pulse until blended. Pour oil through feed tube and pulse until mixture resembles coarse crumbs. Add water, 1 tablespoon at a time, and pulse until dough forms. Flatten dough into disk; wrap in plastic wrap and refrigerate at least 1 hour or up to 3 days.

2 Preheat oven to 375°F. On lightly floured surface, roll dough out to 12-inch circle; ease it into 10-inch deep-dish pie pan, pressing evenly onto bottom and up sides of pan. Prick dough all over with fork. Crimp edges.

3 Line pie crust with foil; fill with pie weights or dried beans. Bake until dough looks dried around edges, about 20 minutes; remove foil and weights. Return crust to oven and bake just until dough is golden, 10–12 minutes longer. Cool crust in pan on rack 10 minutes.

4 Meanwhile, to make filling, combine yams and brown sugar in food processor and pulse until smooth. Add evaporated milk, orange juice, molasses, eggs, egg white, spice, and remaining 1/2 teaspoon salt; pulse until blended. Pour filling into crust. Bake just until center is set, 40–45 minutes. Cool completely on rack. Cut into 12 wedges.

Per serving (1 wedge): 214 Cal, 4 g Fat, 1 g Sat Fat, 0 g Trans Fat, 37 mg Chol, 208 mg Sod, 39 g Carb, 1 g Fib, 5 g Prot, 115 mg Calc. ***POINTS*** value: ***4.***

IN THE KITCHEN

To serve this pie with a delicious garnish of pumpkinseed brittle, spray a 12-inch square of aluminum foil with nonstick spray and set aside. Toast 1/2 cup raw shelled green pumpkinseeds in a small nonstick skillet over medium heat until seeds are golden and popping, about 2 minutes. Add 2 tablespoons maple syrup and a large pinch of salt to the pan; cook, stirring constantly, until the syrup is reduced to a glaze, about 2 minutes. Spread seeds over the foil and cool. Break the brittle into pieces and sprinkle over the pie. This addition will increase the per-serving *POINTS* value by *1.*

COCONUT SHRIMP, PAGE 68; RASPBERRY CHAMPAGNE COCKTAILS, PAGE 67

Index

C

R

S

Recipes by *POINTS* value

0 *POINTS* VALUE

1 *POINTS* VALUE

2 *POINTS* VALUE

3 *POINTS* VALUE

4 *POINTS* VALUE

5 *POINTS* VALUE

6 *POINTS* VALUE

7 *POINTS* VALUE

8 *POINTS* VALUE

Titles in green type represent recipes that work with the Simply Filling technique.

Props generously provided by:
Alex Marshall, alexmarshallstudios.com;
Jasper Conran for Wedgwood, Martha Stewart for Wedgwood, wedgwood.com;
Le Creuset, lecreuset.co.uk;
Spring, springhome.com;
Table Art and LSA, tableartonline.com.

GLUTEN FREE
10 OZ. (284g)

Dry and Liquid Measurement Equivalents

If you are converting the recipes in this book to metric measurements, use the following chart as a guide.

TEASPOONS	TABLESPOONS	CUPS	FLUID OUNCES
3 teaspoons	1 tablespoon		1/2 fluid ounce
6 teaspoons	2 tablespoons	1/8 cup	1 fluid ounce
8 teaspoons	2 tablespoons plus 2 teaspoons	1/6 cup	
12 teaspoons	4 tablespoons	1/4 cup	2 fluid ounces
15 teaspoons	5 tablespoons	1/3 cup minus 1 teaspoon	
16 teaspoons	5 tablespoons plus 1 teaspoon	1/3 cup	
18 teaspoons	6 tablespoons	1/4 cup plus 2 tablespoons	3 fluid ounces
24 teaspoons	8 tablespoons	1/2 cup	4 fluid ounces
30 teaspoons	10 tablespoons	1/2 cup plus 2 tablespoons	5 fluid ounces
32 teaspoons	10 tablespoons plus 2 teaspoons	2/3 cup	
36 teaspoons	12 tablespoons	3/4 cup	6 fluid ounces
42 teaspoons	14 tablespoons	1 cup minus 2 tablespoons	7 fluid ounces
45 teaspoons	15 tablespoons	1 cup minus 1 tablespoon	
48 teaspoons	16 tablespoons	1 cup	8 fluid ounces

OVEN TEMPERATURE

250°F	120°C	400°F	200°C
275°F	140°C	425°F	220°C
300°F	150°C	450°F	230°C
325°F	160°C	475°F	250°C
350°F	180°C	500°F	260°C
375°F	190°C	525°F	270°C

VOLUME

1/4 teaspoon	1 milliliter
1/2 teaspoon	2 milliliters
1 teaspoon	5 milliliters
1 tablespoon	15 milliliters
2 tablespoons	30 milliliters
3 tablespoons	45 milliliters
1/4 cup	60 milliliters
1/3 cup	80 milliliters
1/2 cup	120 milliliters
2/3 cup	160 milliliters
3/4 cup	175 milliliters
1 cup	240 milliliters
1 quart	950 milliliters

LENGTH

1 inch	25 millimeters
1 inch	2.5 centimeters

WEIGHT

1 ounce	30 grams
1/4 pound	120 grams
1/2 pound	240 grams
1 pound	480 grams

Note: Measurement of less than 1/8 teaspoon is considered a dash or a pinch. Metric volume measurements are approximate.

soft sangria

This is a version of the well-known Spanish wine cup that has caught out many an unwary tourist because it seems so innocuous, whereas it is actually very potent. A Soft Sangria poses no such danger of unexpected inebriation, but is just as refreshing and flavorsome. Make sure all the ingredients are thoroughly chilled before mixing them.

SERVES 20

6 cups red grape juice, 1¼ cups orange juice,

3 measures cranberry juice, 2 measures lemon juice, 2 measures lime juice,

4 measures sugar syrup (see page 9), block of ice,

slices of lemon, slices of orange, slices of lime, to decorate

1 Put the grape juice, orange juice, cranberry juice, lemon juice, lime juice, and sugar syrup into a chilled punch bowl and stir well.

2 Add the ice and decorate with the slices of lemon, orange, and lime.

DOWN MEXICO WAY

SANGRITA SECA (to serve 6): pour 2 cups tomato juice, 1 cup orange juice, 3 measures lime juice, ½ measure Tabasco sauce, and 2 teaspoons Worcestershire sauce into a pitcher. Add 1 seeded and finely chopped jalapeño chile. Season to taste with celery salt and freshly ground white pepper and stir well to mix. Cover with plastic wrap and chill in the refrigerator for at least 1 hour. To serve, half fill chilled glasses with cracked ice cubes and strain the cocktail over them.

DID YOU KNOW?

The easiest way to make a large block of ice is to freeze an ordinary ice cube tray filled with water, having first removed the compartments.

Cocktail index